MW00787358

A WHISPER REVIVAL

Our Only Option

To Wendell

2 Corinthian 4:5

A WHISPER REVIVAL

Our Only Option

TIMOTHY WILLIAMS

WINEPRESS WP PUBLISHING

Printed in the United States of America

Published by WinePress Publishing, PO Box 428, Enumclaw, WA 98022.

ISBN 1-57921-274-3
Library of Congress Catalog Card Number: 99-69261

Dedicated to those who love the whisper of God,
rather than the clamor of religious man.

The words of the wise heard in quietness are better
than the shouting of a ruler among fools.
Ecc. 9:17 (NASB)

CONTENTS

Introduction ix

Chapter One — The Whisper Revival 13

Chapter Two — The Cross 21

Chapter Three — Receiving This Revival 25

Chapter Four — A Shameful Thing 31

Chapter Five — Revival Begins 47

Chapter Six — In the Midst of Revival 79

Chapter Seven — The Revival Cry 89

Chapter Eight — Wanting to Help –The Opposition 97

Chapter Nine — Revival Resumed 101

Chapter Ten — The Acid Test 119

Chapter Eleven — The Whole Camp 125

Chapter Twelve — Words of Comfort 137

Chapter Thirteen — The One Thing 143

Chapter Fourteen — Discipleship –To Begin 147

Everything Said 149

Endnotes 151

INTRODUCTION

"You hypocrites!" Jesus exclaimed because the people did not understand the time in which they lived. For each time period that God designed before the world began is unique. Each time period in history poses its own problems and has its own promises. God does this so that each generation will cry out to Him rather than make history their god.[1] Indeed, as you read the New Testament notice how Jesus healed the same illness but used different methods.

So too, each of God's children must understand the time period in which they live so that they are not taken in falseness. This book is about understanding God's last call to revival before all of Hell is let loose.

> And He was also saying to the crowds, "When you see a cloud rising in the west, immediately you say, 'A shower is coming,' and so it turns out. And when you see a south wind blowing, you say, 'It will be a hot day,' and it turns out that way. You hypocrites! You know how to analyze the appearance of the earth and the sky, but why do you not analyze this present time?" (Luke 12:54-56 NASB)

The blessing of revival cannot be gained unless we realize how Jesus is wanting to come to each of us. Failure to realize what will bring us peace today will ensure the destruction of our religious world. Our Jerusalem will be torn down brick by brick.

> When He approached Jerusalem, He saw the city and wept over it, saying, "If you had known in this day, even you, the things which make for peace! But now they have been hidden from your eyes. For the days will come upon you when your enemies will throw up a barricade against you, and surround you and hem you in on every side, and they will level you to the ground and your children within you, and they will not leave in you one stone upon another, because you did not recognize the time of your visitation." (Luke 19:41-44 NASB)

Because the people failed to "recognize the time" of their "visitation" from God and how God wanted to work "peace" in them, they found their religious world totally destroyed in the future. There is much talk of revival these days, but little understanding of the time in which we live and how God desires to offer revival.

For twenty-five years God has closed my mouth, hemmed me in, and refused me opportunity to speak of this. To be sure there was much sin and self in my life which had to be cleansed first, but also to give me time to observe the different waves of revival throughout the land. With my wife, I traveled back and forth across the United States as God led from time to time, watching, praying, and letting God work His wisdom about the situation. It really was His leading and work that led to this book, as I never understood at the time what the purpose was of those trips.

This book will use the shadow of the Old Testament so that we might appreciate the Light of God in our time. We are able to do this because the same "Rock" we have was with them also[1]. Many times in this book you will find a mixture of present day terms used in conjunction with Old Testament ideas. We shall bring out both old and new treasures so that we might be rich in the Lord.

> And Jesus said to them, "Therefore every scribe who has become a disciple of the kingdom of heaven is like a head of a household, who brings out of his treasure things new and old." (Matt. 13:52 NASB)

God longs to bring His people peace and revival in this age, but such waters can only be obtained by letting God come to us on His terms. If you are weary of the noisy false revivals, then praise God. For Jesus comes to you, with His chosen cross for you, to "make[s]" you "lie down in green pastures." He will crucify your restless flesh so that you can drink deep from the reviving "quiet waters."

> He makes me lie down in green pastures; He leads me beside quiet waters. (Ps. 23:2 NASB)

CHAPTER ONE

THE WHISPER REVIVAL

IF YOU WANT REVIVAL, TRUE REVIVAL, IN YOUR LIFE, THERE IS HOPE. A whisper revival is possible. You will have to become very quiet to experience and hold onto it. You will have to quietly surrender all to God in simple humility if you want the Holy Spirit to work this revival in you. You must not look for revival in large groups, but in each individual. And you must know the one thing to look for that shows a true revival is happening.

True revival will not be advertised, promoted, or shouted. It will not come with or because of grand works, loud prayers, and zealous applications of rules and principles. For the very minute you do that, the Holy Spirit will stop the work. It is the "quiet waters" God wants to lead us to. Don't fight the Lord as He tries to lead you to the "quiet waters" where you might be honestly revived.

He makes me lie down in green pastures, he leads me beside quiet waters . . . (Ps. 23:2)

It is a quiet revival that shatters, blesses, and changes one's whole life, but it begins and ends with a whisper. The whisper will totally

13

lay bare all of your church worship, your good deeds, and Christian walk, for it is the revival of 1 Kings. Though you think yourself an Elijah, you too will still hide your face. Even if your ministry is known as one of those tough talking ministries, you will discover you have been leaving out the nails that come with the cross. For after the "fire" of Pentecost, at the start of the new church, comes the "gentle whisper" to the end time church

> The Lord said, "Go out and stand on the mountain in the presence of the Lord, for the Lord is about to pass by." Then a great and powerful wind tore the mountains apart and shattered the rocks before the Lord, but the Lord was not in the wind. After the wind there was an earthquake, but the Lord was not in the earthquake. After the earthquake came a fire, but the Lord was not in the fire. *And after the fire came a gentle whisper.* When Elijah heard it, he pulled his cloak over his face and went out and stood at the mouth of the cave. Then a voice said to him, "What are you doing here, Elijah?" (1 Kings 19:11-13 NASB, emphasis added)

> Even if your ministry is known as one of those tough talking ministries, you will discover you have been leaving out the nails that come with the cross.

For too long the church has deluded itself into thinking it stands on holy ground. Everything around us is so wicked, it is easy to look holy in Sodom or compared to Jezebel.

Like Elijah, the church looks for God in earthquakes, fire, wind, and the shattering of rocks. They believe themselves to be the only ones not defiled, because they cannot see the hidden servants of God. Like Elijah, they are too busy looking at the loud and flashy things in the church to notice the 7,000 that have not bowed to self. Like Elijah, they think they are so correct, so on fire in the Lord, that they do not realize they are where they should not be. They are blind to that fact that they too have fallen prey to the loud works and strivings of the flesh. Like Elijah, God is asking the church of today how it got where it is. In other words, "What are you doing here...?"

> We cannot change the times we live in, but we can understand them by God's grace.

If you want eyes that are opened to see those hidden in God, then you must listen for the whisper of God. If you want to fellowship with those who are of God in our time, then you must sit down and be quiet with them as they worship the Lord. For this whisper revival brings quiet and sober worship. Again, the times in which we live do not permit God to bring any other kind of revival.

Our Time Period

It takes wisdom to understand the making of a whisper revival—wisdom about the times we live in. We must become men who know "what Israel should do" from understanding "the times" in which we live.

> . . . *men of Issachar, who understood the times and knew what Israel should do*—200 *chiefs, with all their relatives under their command;* . . . (1 Chron. 12:32, emphasis added)

We cannot change the times we live in, but we can understand them by God's grace. We cannot force God to do anything, but we can understand what God will do in our time.

So many people want revival and seek, with great zeal, to achieve it. The hunger for revival is so great that men are willing to claim anything as revival. Year after year something new comes along that the church places the stamp of revival on. Churches use the term revival to increase attendance and ministries use it to promote their agendas. Indeed, the great contest hidden in men's heart today is who can top the other "Christian" with tales of victory and miracles. After all, when was the last time you heard someone share how the cross was humbling him and taking more of his life away? We are bored with stories of escapes in a basket.[1]

> Everywhere today men talk and hope for revival but refuse the only kind of revival that God offers in our time.

Everywhere today men talk and hope for revival but refuse the only kind of revival that God offers in our time. How few there are who understand "what Israel should do" in order to be revived and overcoming in God. This is the current false revival that God warned us would take place in the last days.[2]

NOT POSSIBLE

We must come to understand that, because of the times we live in, a large scale, emotionally charged revival is not possible. We live in the last days when the love of most will grow cold. We live on the verge of total world breakdown, the coming of the anti-Christ, and so the kind of revival that men are looking for is just not possible. Wickedness has increased in the church to such a degree that a fiery, wind-like, earth shattering revival is not in God's will. Just look at the fruit of all the fiery "revivals" and self-promoted statements of "revival" with God's eyes and you will understand why.

> Because of the increase of wickedness, the love of most will grow cold, but he who stands firm to the end will be saved. (Matt. 24:12-13)

Indeed, Satan is about to be let loose on earth and the church's power is about to be broken.[3] Therefore, the style of revival everyone is looking for is just not in God's plan and the wise will understand. If you understand the times in which we live, then you know that the following Scripture is impossible to claim.

> If you hear any ministry, preacher, or book claim this promise, then you know they are not speaking by the power of the Holy Spirit. . . . For such a revival of the people and the land is not possible. It will not be possible until Jesus returns.

> . . . if my people, who are called by my name, will humble themselves and pray and seek my face and turn from their wicked ways, then will I hear from heaven and will forgive their sin and will heal their land. (2 Chron. 7:14)

If you hear any ministry, preacher, or book claim this promise, then you know they are not speaking by the power of the Holy Spirit. They prophesy their own desires, not that of God's will and plan.

Indeed, they are not wise and have no clue as to the times in which we live. For such a revival of the people and the land is not possible. It will not be possible until Jesus returns.

HIDDEN SERVANTS

Be sure of this, God has those who are His, but you can't find them because you are at the wrong place doing the wrong religious things. You are so noisy with your opinions, doctrines, works, dancing, music, and activity that you can't see the sin that needs to be dealt with. You are unable to fellowship with those whom God has reserved for Himself because you are so busy blessing yourself in the name of the Lord. Like Elijah, we are so happy with our religions walk we don't even bother to ask God who the 7,000 are that we might fellowship with them.

We are so self-satisfied and self-sufficient in the Lord that even when we are shown our sin like Elijah was, we don't ask God to reveal His true believers. How many there are who are content to sit at home because they think no church is worthy of them. They are content and satisfied with themselves because they rebuke others. If we really understood the crucified life, we would beg God to show us who the 7,000 are so that we might break bread with them—because those who walk this walk are very lonely, few, and precious in the Lord. They are the ministries and individuals who are last in the church but will be first in heaven.

> Yet I reserve seven thousand in Israel—all whose knees have not bowed down to Baal and all whose mouths have not kissed him. (1 Kings 19:18)

Everyday one hears new tales of miraculous and noisy revivals, but the Lord is not in them. Stand before the Lord, be quiet and you will know that the Lord is not in the current "earthquake" or fiery revival. Nor is the Lord in the "great" and "powerful" "wind" that is shattering the "rocks." Understand the times: if a revival is newsworthy, it is not of God. If the revival can be promoted, merchandise sold, announced, and influenced, it is not of God. The only revival that God is working right now is one that is a "whisper."

CHAPTER TWO

THE CROSS

THE WHISPER REVIVAL CENTERS AROUND ONE THING AND REMAINS there. As you look at the church, you see men become excited about all kinds of things in Jesus. Ministries become devoted to a cause, individuals burn with a passion over an issue and promote topics as if they were the most important thing in Jesus. The issues are too numerous to list. They range from home schooling or public school; in politics or out of politics; established church buildings or home churches; TV or no TV; KJV only or NIV; spiritual gifts or no gifts and so on. But the one and *only* thing that every Christian and church should burn with and preach is missing today. That one thing is the cross.

> For I resolved to know nothing while I was with you except Jesus
> Christ and him crucified. (1 Cor. 2:2)

By cross, we of course do not mean the shallow preaching that is proclaimed. We mean a cross that deals powerfully with self and one's life, and that can wrestle to death any issue—a cross so powerful, it is the only issue. The whisper revival is a renewal of understanding what it means to hate[1] for Jesus and of counting that cost. A whisper revival brings forth a "resolve" to stay at the cross in every situation. And it does take "resolve" not to be moved by all the causes, opinions, and works going on in the name of the Lord. It takes "resolve" from the Holy Spirit to see clearly with each person we meet, with every doctrine that is confronted, and with every work that is done in Jesus' name, that the cross that crucifies self is the only answer.

> If you listen to the whisper of God, you too will pull your "cloak" over your "face."

Consider the sermons and songs you hear, the books and magazines you read: do they end in and start with the cross? A whisper revival is God opening our dull minds and hard hearts again to the power of the cross in a man's life.[2] How much time is being wasted, how much debate and argument is happening, and how much sin is in the church today because men refuse to be resolved to know nothing but Jesus Christ and Him crucified.

DEATH TO SELF

If you listen to the whisper of God, you too will pull your religious "cloak" over your "face." You who truly desire revival will be put on a cross and exposed and you will seek to cover yourself. You will be ashamed and blessed at the same time if you submit to God's revival in these the last days. You will learn what it is to "always carry around in [y]our body the death of Jesus" so that you might have His "life."

> We always carry around in our body the death of Jesus, so that the life of Jesus may also be revealed in our body. (2 Cor. 4:10)

All the false revivals taking place in the Lord today have one thing in common. They feed the flesh of man and puff him up in self-righteousness. Even the revivals that look like individuals are cleaning up their lives are a sham. The result is always that self, religious self, or the church is lifted up in pride. You might be asking how one can know this. We know this because of the advertisement, promotion, pride, gimmicks, and shallow doctrine associated with these revivals. The Holy Spirit will make this clear if you will die to self.

Like Adam and Eve, to whom Satan made promises if they would only serve him, these individuals are promised great things if they will worship the false revival. The miracles that happen to them are the blessings and things of this world.[3] They are the false miracles that God promised would be worked in the last days. Indeed, the positive changes in their lives are the same changes all men in the world can make. To be sure, changes are made, but self is still fully alive. It is the same wisdom that gave Adam and Eve the power to change their lives in the Garden of Eden. Their changes do not come from the hopelessness that only the Holy Spirit can work. It is instead a renewal by the strength of man. Their revival is only a "renewal" by the "strength" of religious man.

> You were wearied by all your ways, but you would not say, "It is hopeless." You found renewal of your strength, and so you did not faint. (Isa. 57:10)

The one thing that shows a revival to be of God is not present. That thing is the cross of Christ in each person's life. People are not increasing in the very foundational things every day that bring death to self and hatred in Jesus.[4]

The man who loves his life will lose it, while the man who hates his life in this world will keep it for eternal life. (John 12:25)

CHAPTER THREE

RECEIVING
THIS REVIVAL

T O EXPERIENCE THE ONLY REVIVAL THAT GOD OFFERS IN THESE TIMES, you must do several things.

First and foremost you must choose wisely who you listen to. The loud, emotional "revivalist" must be fully and *completely* rejected. Don't even bother to attend a revival meeting. For if they promote it as such, God is not in it.

You must pray and ask the Lord who is preaching the "quiet words" that only the "wise" in Him are given. Make no mistake about it, God is not giving these flamboyant preachers His wisdom; they are only promoting themselves.

> The quiet words of the wise are more to be heeded than the shouts
> of a ruler of fools. (Ecc. 9:17)

The loud, noisy, and emotionally charged church must be left. The successful church and Christian must be rejected in favor of the poor church.[1]

Now there lived in that city a man poor but wise, and he saved the city by his wisdom. But nobody remembered that poor man. So I said, "Wisdom is better than strength." But the poor man's wisdom is despised, and his words are no longer heeded. (Ecc. 9:15-16)

You must listen to the one who is "despised" and whose words no one heeds. For like Jesus, the preachers that are of God in these, the last days, are the quiet ones.

Here is my servant, whom I uphold, my chosen one in whom I delight; I will put my Spirit on him and he will bring justice to the nations. He will not shout or cry out, or raise his voice in the streets. (Isa. 42:1-2)

You must get your eyes off of the powerful church and see the church of the poor widow. You must attend the "First Church of the Widow" if you want the only true revival that is being offered by God today. For not one, not a single stone of these revivals that have been built will remain. Indeed, when all the revival rocks have been thrown down and the dust has settled, it will be the poor widow whom Jesus will be holding in His arms. Then you will wish you had been worshipping and fellowshipping with her. Though your revival be "adorned with beautiful stones" be assured of this—it will be torn down. Every last stone will be "torn down."

As he looked up, Jesus saw the rich putting their gifts into the temple treasury. He also saw a poor widow put in two very small copper coins. "I tell you the truth," he said, "this poor widow has put in more than all the others. All these people gave their gifts out of their wealth; but she out of her poverty put in all she had to live on." Some of his disciples were remarking about how the temple was adorned with beautiful stones and with gifts dedicated to God. But Jesus said, "As for what you see here, the time will come when not one stone will be left on another; every one of them will be thrown down." (Luke 21:1-6)

HATING YOUR OWN LIFE

To experience God's revival, you must be willing to be taught to hate your own life, pick up a cross, and follow Jesus. This kind of discipleship is a quiet, step by step following of the Holy Spirit. Indeed, with each passing day, quietness only increases and sin is deafened by this silence. With each step being one more denying of self and dying to sin, the soul becomes more

> You must get your eyes off of the powerful church and see the church of the poor widow.

and more quiet.[2] It is a suffering with Jesus so that you no longer please yourself or do "what you want" to do.[3]

> For the sinful nature desires what is contrary to the Spirit, and the Spirit what is contrary to the sinful nature. They are in conflict with each other, so that you do not do what you want. But if you are led by the Spirit, you are not under law. (Gal. 5:17-18)

Such a walk that is "led of the Spirit" works much quietness and soberness.[4] It is a daily revival by the whisper of God that causes one to hide his face from the power of God that is working in his life. You will be humbled and amazed, weeping, and rejoicing. You will be both rejoicing and trembling, for there is no revival like this revival by the whisper of God! For God will work Psalm 2:11 in your life.

> Serve the Lord with fear and rejoice with trembling. (Ps. 2:11)

How many there are who reject the true revival of God today because they refuse to stop and listen to His whisper. They will not give God time and refuse to wait on Him to work.[5] They are too busy worshipping to allow God to do His work in them.

As it was in Isaiah's day, so it is today. Most reject the quiet whisper of God in favor of the activity of religious man. How they love the power of their "horses" and activity.

> This is what the Sovereign Lord, the Holy One of Israel, says: "In repentance and rest is your salvation, in quietness and trust is your strength, but you would have none of it. You said, 'No, we will flee on horses.' Therefore you will flee! You said, 'We will ride off on swift horses.' Therefore your pursuers will be swift!" (Isa. 30:15-16)

> God will laugh at them when they cry out for mercy. For long ago they rejected the quiet way of the cross for the noise of man's religion.

Such individuals need to repent, because soon their sin will catch up with them. Soon their "pursuers" will come in great swiftness and they will not escape. That sin they think they are holding back with all of their zeal will pursue and overtake them. Only this time, it will not let go. Then, although they cry out to the Lord for help, even rejecting all of their revival ways, God will not answer to heal them. Indeed, God will laugh at them when they cry out for mercy. For long ago they rejected the quiet way of the cross for the noise of man's religion.

> I in turn will laugh at your disaster; I will mock when calamity overtakes you—when calamity overtakes you like a storm, when

disaster sweeps over you like a whirlwind, when distress and trouble overwhelm you. Then they will call to me but I will not answer; they will look for me but will not find me. Since they hated knowledge and did not choose to fear the Lord, since they would not accept my advice and spurned my rebuke, they will eat the fruit of their ways and be filled with the fruit of their schemes. (Prov. 1:26-31)

No Advertisement

If God should begin to whisper to you, and you should begin to experience God's revival, do not advertise it the way others now proclaim revival. Allow no insanity in your life or church.[6] Quietly share what good God is working in your life, one on one with each person. Invite them to come *down* to your level and lose all of their pride and self. Invite them to meet you at the foot of the cross, in all the humility that they will allow the Holy Spirit to work in them. But do not advertise and do not promote your church. Do not seek to stylize the gospel by the dress, actions, and clamor of the world. If you do, God will stop the work and you will be left to make up for the void with your own emotions and works. Share only with others who are willing to quietly sit down with you and talk about the power of the whisper of God. Do not throw your pearls to pigs. Understand the times we live in and you will not fall prey to the nonsense that is sweeping the land. Though you might think yourself a king in the Lord, go and listen to the quiet wise men of today who understand the times we live in. Do this and rich revival will be yours.

> Since it was customary for the king to consult experts in matters of law and justice, he spoke with the *wise men who understood the times* . . . (Esther 1:13, emphasis added)

CHAPTER FOUR

A SHAMEFUL THING

My dear children, for whom I am again in the pains of childbirth
until Christ is formed in you . . . (Gal. 4:19)

AS THE PASSAGE ABOVE DECLARES, REVIVAL RESEMBLES THE PAINFUL
process of childbirth. As we will see from Scripture, revival
requires labor, anxiety, and time.

True revival gains back what we have lost and renews what we
forfeited because of sinful behavior. The state of needing revival
denotes a thing of shame. While all servants need refreshing times
in the Lord, those who need revival need reconciliation with God.
Revival belongs to those who have left the church, been trapped in
sin, or have been sent by God into captivity because of their stubborn refusal to repent. Anyone who over a long period of time ignores most of God's Word in favor of their opinions and church
dogma will find revival necessary. Certainly, revival demonstrates
God's loving-kindness poured out, but it is shameful for any church
or man to need revival.

Jesus never needed revival, but walked continually in the presence of God, showing the "same diligence to the end."[3] We, on the other hand, are so prone to give in to our sin, that we force ourselves into a place where revival provides the only solution. The command, "Never be lacking in zeal, but keep your spiritual fervor, serving the Lord,"[2] should be our walk every day, all day. When we fail to obey this scripture long enough in our lives, by the power of the Holy Spirit revival must occur for reconciliation with God. Any church that advertises that they plan a revival only adds to their sin and shameful conduct before Christ.

> Revival is His work and He will not give it at the command of man. Revival, after all, brings a renewal of knowing God as God.

One can no more predict which way the wind will blow, than one can predict when and if revival winds will blow.

> The wind blows where it wishes and you hear the sound of it, but do not know where it comes from and where it is going; so is everyone who is born of the Spirit. (John 3:8 NASB)

God makes it clear that no man can predict the revival winds that cause men to regain the New Life in Christ again. Revival is His work and He will not give it at the command of man. Revival, after all, brings a renewal of knowing God as God.

> As you do not know the path of the wind, or how the body is formed in a mother's womb, so you cannot understand the work of God, the Maker of all things. (Ecc. 11:5)

Christians today hold a strong false belief that God will send a revival upon millions in the Last Days. In reality, only a false revival on such a scale will take place by the hand of God. However, that doesn't mean that a few might experience true revival. In fact, only a few experience renewal because God only gives revival to the remnant. Revival never comes to new converts. They merely have a conversion experience that the Holy Spirit works in those whom God seeks to begin the New Life. Revival restores the New Life in those that abused redemption after receiving it. Revival means labor pains all over again.

We will examine the book of Ezra to see how God's true revival takes place. This way we will be not be taken in by the current revival craze sweeping the church. For there lies a vast contrast between what happens around us today and true Godly revival.

THOSE IN NEED OF REVIVAL

Many individuals don't even realize they desperately need revival—they are too dead spiritually to know their condition. Revival is for those who have read the Bible for years but remain entrenched in their opinions and/or church dogma. These kinds of individuals, of whom there are many, feel totally devastated when God tries to bring revival into their lives. When this happens, everything that they based their Christian walk on is torn down. This can be expected by anyone who has led a Christian life but has not experienced the pain and power of the cross in their life.

The truth is, most enjoy the desert Christian life. They have become so accustomed to their dead spiritual lives and rebuffing the Spirit's rebukes, that they believe that the desert is the glorified Christian life. Their lives are so full of spiritual flesh and pride that they feel little need for the Holy Spirit any longer. Yet they think they are alive in Jesus. They remain satisfied with their little spiritual lives. Therefore they refuse to humble themselves enough to really repent. They feel so content with what they can get from God, or the little ways they choose to repent, that the true life of Jesus doesn't interest them any longer. Because God's Spirit has been silent for so long, they have filled the void with other religious and worldly activities and goals. They simply stay too busy in the world or church to give God time to speak, and it would do God little good to speak anyway. Since they have quieted the Holy Spirit with their lies about how they do not sin, they can only hear their own voice justifying religious self.

> Since the parents raised them in captivity, claiming that the Lord blessed them, their children never experience the sweetness of true fellowship with the Lord and never see the resurrected life in their parents.

People in captivity drag their children with them. This causes God to send revival in the lives of the children. Since the parents raised them in captivity, claiming that the Lord blessed them, their children never experience the sweetness of true fellowship with the Lord and never see the resurrected life in their parents. They think that the unrighteous deeds and self-justifications of their parents constitute the Christian life. They never see their parents surrender everything to God, but only live the Christian life on their own terms.

If parents continually confess failure and never gain the victory over self from a totally surrendered heart, the children will despise their parents' words. Despise means to regard as unworthy of one's interest or concern.

... Do not let anyone despise you. (Titus 2:15b)

Indeed, these children have no reason to listen to their parents. They will grow up to despise their parents and have little reason to discuss righteousness with them. As Proverbs 10:20 says, though such parents love their children with all their hearts, it is of "little value."

The tongue of the righteous is choice silver, but the heart of the wicked is of little value. (Prov. 10:20)

God must then revive the children to straighten out what the parents twisted concerning the character of God. After all, a child's first and main impression of God is his parents. If a parent's religion bends God to their own will and wishes, the children will also form God into an idol. If the cross that bends us to God's will is not present, our children trust in a false Christianity.

If children sense that their parents seem powerless over self, then they will consider Christianity a worthless religion. If they see hypocrisy, they too will think they can live the same way and yet be saved in the end.[3]

When the Lord tries to come to the children, they do not understand who He is, or feel the need for Him, because their parents have deceived them. It is always amazing to watch someone go into captivity. Even the destruction of their children does not cause parents to repent. As in Jeremiah's day, they were more willing to eat their children than to love the Lord by way of the crucified life.[4] A child in such a situation will more than likely need revival rather than just be able to quietly grow up in the Lord. As we shall see in Ezra, the young men will rejoice while the old men cry. The old men weep because of opportunities wasted in their lives. The young men will rejoice because God restores what their parents twisted and destroyed. How sad that those hindered in their walk with God hold back others.

He who heeds discipline shows the way to life, but whoever ignores correction leads others astray. (Prov. 10:17)

> To those spiritually starved in captivity, even the bitter spiritual things of captivity can seem "sweet" to them in the Lord.

The more spiritually dead someone becomes, the more they and others think their little acts of righteousness are alive—much as when someone is on their death bed, we talk of them as "doing much better." Those who are spiritually dead become callused to their sin. Sin is such a normal state of affairs that they become hardened to conviction. With each step into self, they begin to think of their sin as part of every day life. They even think their sin is of Jesus.

To those spiritually starved in captivity, even the bitter spiritual things of captivity can seem "sweet" to them in the Lord. They feel thankful for any attention God might give, even a rebuke. Although they don't really repent from the heart, rebukes make them feel okay spiritually. They're like spoiled brats that thrive on any attention, even negative attention. What they consider "sweet" in the Lord becomes spiritually twisted. Bitter works appear sweet and holy to them. Their deeds are not complete before Jesus, but like the church in Sardis, they think they are "alive."

> He who is full loathes honey, but to the hungry even what is bitter tastes sweet. (Prov. 27:7)

Those "full" in the Lord can see even the sweetest acts of the worldly as loathsome. They want nothing to do with that kind of honey. They become weary of the double-minded, who have one eye on the Lord's will and another eye on self.

When those in captivity look at themselves and their Christian walk, they believe that short lived acts of repentance and good works suffice. They even feel satisfied when God works in their lives. In reality, God works in their lives because He must, not because He finds them worthy to glorify His name in greater ways. In short, captives have little clue of their desperate need of revival because they have grown "accustomed" to a "desert" kind of Christian life. As the passage below states, they protest their innocence and feel familiar with the desert.

> How can you say, "I am not defiled; I have not run after the Baals"? See how you behaved in the valley; consider what you have done. You are a swift she-camel running here and there, a wild donkey accustomed to the desert, sniffing the wind in her craving—in her heat who can restrain her? Any males that pursue her need not tire themselves; at mating time they will find her. (Jer. 2:23-24)

Very often those who need revival are the last to admit or to see how desperately they need it. They boast, (verse 23), "I am not defiled" and have all manner of excuses when God confronts their sin.

They are the type who are always being crucified to a sin, but never die to it. Self, the root of sin, reigns on the throne in their hearts even as they deny specific aspects of self. Let us each come before the Lord with holy trembling and ask Him how much self has really been put to "death" by the Holy Spirit.

> For if you live according to the sinful nature, you will die; but if by the Spirit you put to death the misdeeds of the body, you will live. (Rom. 8:13)

Often those who need revival remain satisfied with the sparse grass they find in the desert to eat. They feel satisfied with short moments of repentance and comfort from God's Word. These are the type who believe they will love the Lord even when He sends them into captivity. They believe that if they hang around God and endure the discipline, God must accept them in the end. They forget that others perished in the "desert" and that "without holiness no one will see the Lord." They forget that though they endured the forty years of discipline, God swore that they would "never enter" His "rest."

> So, as the Holy Spirit says: "Today, if you hear his voice, do not harden your hearts as you did in the rebellion, during the time of testing in the desert, where your fathers tested and tried me and for forty years saw what I did. That is why I was angry with that generation, and I said, 'Their hearts are always going astray, and they have not known my ways.' So I declared on oath in my anger, 'They shall never enter my rest.' " See to it, brothers, that none of you has a sinful, unbelieving heart that turns away from the living God. (Heb. 3:7-12)

Make every effort to live in peace with all men and to be holy; without holiness no one will see the Lord. (Heb. 12:14)

After their stubbornness sent them into captivity, they grew more stubborn about their need to repent. God sent them into captivity because of their stubbornness. It was a desperate act of love on God's part, for He hoped they might wake up and cry out to Him.

> Sadly, most captives grow accustomed to the desert rather than repent with a full and total heart.

Sadly, most captives grow accustomed to the desert rather than repent with a full and total heart. Instead they become a "swift she-camel running here and there," changing in one area, seeking God in another way, changing their words and garments "here and there," but never really surrendering self. They do one "Christian" thing after another, but never really follow the Spirit all the way in all things. When God starts to revive them, their stubbornness checks it and He must wait for another time to try. Alas, they put their souls in great danger and may pass the point of no return.

> Revival belongs to anyone who has been out of step with the Spirit long enough that God had to send them into captivity or the desert.

This truth explains why anyone who needs revival must realize it will take years of repentance for full reconciliation with God and for God to correct the wrongs they committed. They must allow the Spirit to search them for sin, stubbornness, and stiff-neckedness as never before—because the last time

God tried to bring them to repentance, they grew rebellious, cold, and dead.

Revival belongs to anyone who has been out of step with the Spirit long enough that God had to send them into captivity or the desert. Anyone who has, over the years, rejected the many calls of the Spirit to repent over "little" things needs revival. Those who continue to out-maneuver the Holy Spirit in the matter of repentance need revival desperately. They are always repenting without giving themselves fully to the Lord. Those who continually ask for forgiveness but never really change, should cry for revival. These people please all the flesh they can and hang on to what is considered "freedom" in the Lord to do. They call God "friend" but make every provision for the flesh.

> Have you not just called to me: "My Father, my friend from my youth, will you always be angry? Will your wrath continue forever?" This is how you talk, but you do all the evil you can. (Jer. 3:4-5)

Those in desperate need for revival falsely believe they try hard to follow after God and have an elevated opinion of their importance in Christ. They usually think they can be a blessing to others even though they remain spiritually dead themselves. They always believe they "confessed" their sins and made real efforts to change. As verse 1 states below, they think they have a reputation of being "alive," or at least somewhat well in Christ.

And to the angel of the church in Sardis write: He who has the seven Spirits of God, and the seven stars, says this: "I know your deeds, that you have a name, that you are alive, but you are dead. Wake up, and strengthen the things that remain, which were about to die; for I have not found your deeds completed in the sight of My God. Remember therefore what you have received and heard; and keep it, and repent. If therefore you will not wake up, I will come like a thief, and you will not know at what hour I will come upon you. But you have a few people in Sardis who have not soiled their garments; and they will walk with Me in white; for they are worthy. He who overcomes shall thus be clothed in white garments; and I will not erase his name from the book of life, and I will confess his name before My Father, and before His angels." (Rev. 3:1-5)

Captivity is the last stage before one falls away completely from the Lord.[5] As Revelation above stated, they are "dead," and "about to die." They still do "deeds" for God, but not "complete" deeds, so Jesus will remove them in short order. They still pray, share the gospel, give money, study the Word, get quiet times, agree with the Spirit and the message of the cross, but their deeds are not "complete." They are still too full of self. They have simply become fools with a message. Their wisdom and works in Christ just kind of "hang" there not really going anywhere. There is no real power in what they are doing and it always falls short.

> Like a lame man's legs that hang limp is a proverb in the mouth of a fool. (Prov. 26:7)

Their words of wisdom are like a "thornbush" in a "drunkard's hand"; they are unable to feel or sense the harm they are doing. Their act of sharing righteousness with others does more harm than good. Since they have no feeling of doing harm, they are proud of their work in God and are shocked when someone points out how harmful their advice on actions were. Indeed, they have an excuse for every failure and mistake, even claim the blood of Jesus. Just as an alcoholic justifies his drinking and will not admit to the problem.

> Like a thornbush in a drunkard's hand is a proverb in the mouth of a fool. (Prov. 26:9)

That is how close they are to the end of their walk in the Lord – and their deeds prove it. Indeed, most will perish in captivity while a very small part of the remnant remains. As we shall see, even that small remnant must be tested and purified. Although they seem dead, there remains something small still alive in them, so hope remains. Yet they stand on the verge of damnation and must "overcome" the self that caused God to give them over to captivity in the first place. They are in great danger and about to die.

The solution is to "wake up." Revival means "waking up" in Christ again. To revive yourself in Christ means you "wake up" and see the reality of who you are in Jesus. Of course waking up, or revival, involves "remembering" what you once "heard" and had once "received," "keep[ing] it" and not letting go of it again by "repenting."

The reason God does not seem able to move with revival in so many lives is because they will not respond to His call. They cannot,

> Revival must come to anyone who let go of the cross and moved out of step with the Holy Spirit over a long period of time.

as Revelation 3:6 states, "hear what the Spirit says."

> He who has an ear, let him hear what the Spirit says to the
> churches. (Rev. 3:6)

Revival must come to anyone who let go of the cross and moved out of step with the Holy Spirit over a long period of time. Usually it was not a moment of one big sin that sent them out into the desert. It was the small, deliberate, unrepentant sins that slowly sent them away. It was a hundred ignorings of the soft voice of the Holy Spirit that caused God to take desperate measures.

Such people cannot really hear God's voice. They only hear echoes of the Spirit's voice from the past and leach off others for spiritual power. Because of their spiritual poverty, they become mockers in quick order. Mockers who mimic just the right spiritual words while they please the flesh. Indeed, they become so good at it that lies and half-truths pour forth from their lips. They have to lie in order to make self look spiritual. Many have lied so much that they believe themselves spiritual and struggling along just fine in the Lord. In short, they believe their own lies. Be careful not to call your "darkness," "light." What a dreadful condition to be in. Make sure you do not focus your eyes on yourself and your words. Make sure they are fixed on Jesus and His powerful crucifying cross.

> But if your eyes are bad, your whole body will be full of darkness.
> If then the light within you is darkness, how great is that darkness! (Matt. 6:23)

Don't delay when He starts to blow revival winds your way. You may never have another chance to repent. Indeed, your total spiritual death will come "like a thief, and you will not know at what hour [it] will come upon you" (Rev. 3:3).

Anyone who keeps repenting of the same old basic self and sins over and over again needs revival. As Hebrews says, anyone who continually "lays a foundation" for repentance of the same old sins, desperately needs revival.

> Therefore let us leave the elementary teachings about Christ and go on to maturity, not laying again the foundation of repentance from acts that lead to death, . . . (Heb. 6:1)

> ## Anyone who keeps repenting of the same old basic self and sins over and over again needs revival.

Anyone in this condition after years in the Lord had better get revival started today. Otherwise they stand in danger of being burned in hell. They have received the blessed rains of God but their hearts are double-minded. They don't despise money, they lie about themselves, and remain unloving and self-absorbed. The bottom line is, if self stays that alive after years in the Lord, a person remains in danger of being "cursed."

> But land that produces thorns and thistles is worthless and is in danger of being cursed. In the end it will be burned. (Heb. 6:8)

If you fit any of these areas, time runs short and you had better stop everything and beg for revival from God.

A QUICK SUMMARY

As we explore the book of Ezra, the following points will become clear as to what constitutes a true, Godly revival.

1. No advertisement can announce or predict a coming revival.
2. It takes years for revival to be completed.
3. Revival stirs a growing and deepening realization of sin.
4. Revival never lasts one day or a weekend.
5. True revival renews interest and obedience of scripture.
6. Revival causes much judging and division to take place.
7. Worship and other religious activities completely stop at times.
8. A renewed interest in the needs of Jesus occurs.
9. Joy mixed with weeping can last for days in a true revival.
10. Above all, revival is marked by sacrifice on our part.
11. Unity is honest and real.
12. The revival cry must be present.
13. After many have fallen away, revival is reserved for the "remnant."
14. Revival consists of a lot of hard work.

THE SIGNS OF A FALSE REVIVAL

Look for the following symptoms of a false revival as you read through the scriptures.

1. The church or ministry advertises revival—they even sell revival merchandise.
2. The revival meeting only lasts for a few days or weeks.
3. The revival preachers promotes himself/herself as a revival preacher.

4. The emotion of the revival generates from persuasive words, stories, and a style of preaching.

5. Conviction of sin is shallow and not followed by outward repentance and a change in the heart.

6. No person is judged. No one removes unclean evil things from their homes and the church.

7. Entertainment occurs, instead of very serious Bible study.

8. Sacrifice never increases.

9. The revival starts with one big bang, rather than increasing slowly over time.

10. Worship services are not canceled for a time period with the Holy Spirit stopping and starting them.

11. Every church doctrine and ministry is not re-evaluated and cleaned up by the power of the Holy Spirit.

12. No new commands are discovered or obeyed.

13. There is no revival "cry" present.

14. The people are always being crucified to sin, but never die totally to self.

CHAPTER FIVE

REVIVAL BEGINS

R EVIVAL ALWAYS STARTS QUIETLY, SLOWLY, AND INCREASES IN INTENSITY over a period of time. Let us quote Ezra 1:1-3, noting how God announces a coming revival.

> Now in the first year of Cyrus king of Persia, in order to fulfill the word of the Lord by the mouth of Jeremiah, the Lord stirred up the spirit of Cyrus king of Persia, so that he sent a proclamation throughout all his kingdom, and also put it in writing, saying, "Thus says Cyrus king of Persia, 'The Lord, the God of heaven, has given me all the kingdoms of the earth, and He has appointed me to build Him a house in Jerusalem, which is in Judah. Whoever there is among you of all His people, may his God be with him! Let him go up to Jerusalem which is in Judah, and rebuild the house of the Lord, the God of Israel; He is the God who is in Jerusalem.' " (Ezra 1:1-3 NASB)

Do you see how quietly the Lord made the revival announcement? God's call to revival is really a "proclamation" to come and work. Indeed, it almost sounds like it mocks revival. For the king said, "May his God be with him!" However, the people know they entered captivity because God hid His face from them. A response to this kind of call for revival will take a genuine response to the Spirit of God. Advertising or promoting revival provokes God to stop it. Normally this happens and the church has to fill the void with their emotions. As you read through the New Testament, notice how Jesus would often say, "Don't tell anyone about this miracle." Indeed, the only time Jesus tells someone to "go and tell" is when the people don't want Him around.[1]

> Hype did not motivate the people to come to a revival so that they might be blessed.

See that you don't tell this to anyone. But go, show yourself to the priest and offer the sacrifices that Moses commanded for your cleansing, as a testimony to them. (Mark 1:44 NASB)

Hype did not motivate the people to come to a revival so that they might be blessed. Jesus[2] never hyped the people and Peter learned this lesson well. See below how Peter sends everyone out of the room when he is going to raise someone from the dead. Jesus had done the same thing and so would he. This was to be no circus or miracle revival meeting. How wicked the church is today. For it invites everyone in the room. It promotes revival with all the pompt self can muster.

Peter went with them, and when he arrived he was taken upstairs to the room. All the widows stood around him, crying and showing him the robes and other clothing that Dorcas had made while she was still with them. Peter sent them all out of the room; then he got down on his knees and prayed. Turning toward the dead woman, he said, "Tabitha, get up." She opened her eyes, and seeing Peter she sat up. (Acts 9:39-40)

In Ezra 1:1-3, the king's summons humiliated the people. It reminded them of Jerusalem's condition, that the temple lay in ruins, and the kind of God who disciplined them. The call to revival by God increasingly crushes our pride and self-righteousness. If a godly preacher calls the people to revival, they will at first shrink back knowing that true revival exposes more of their sin.

The call in Ezra did not entertain the people in the name of the Lord. Not a single aspect of this call promised the people anything. The priest made no promises of healing or miracles. They posted no announcements of special speakers and never preached a "persuasive" word.[3] Instead, this revival called the people to work, to sacrifice and to labor at repen-

> Since revival calls people to serve, rather than to be served by God, it begins with sacrifice.

tance. Since the Israelites' sin had destroyed the temple, only their repentance could rebuild it. The only joy at this point was the grand privilege to once again be allowed to build the church. Their joy did not result from obtaining anything from God, but in the supreme freedom to once again be able to "serve Him without fear."

. . . to rescue us from the hand of our enemies, and *to enable us to serve him without fear* in holiness and righteousness before him all our days. (Luke 1:74-75, emphasis added)

Since revival calls people to serve, rather than to be served by God, it begins with sacrifice. The "survivor" of God's discipline will hear the call to come with sacrifices. This, of course, must include a "freewill offering," for in the past they served God because they knew they must in order to receive His blessings. Like those who followed Jesus only for what they could get from Him, they want to repent of such attitudes.[4] The attitude of wanting something from God caused them to fall into need of revival in the first place.

> . . . every survivor, at whatever place he may live, let the men of that place support him with silver and gold, with goods and cattle, together with a freewill offering for the house of God which is in Jerusalem. (Ezra 1:4)

Therefore, revival begins with the sacrificing of our most precious things—"gold," "silver," "cattle" and "goods"—along with "freewill offerings." In other words, revival returns the people to the words of Jesus, who said that we must give up "everything" and freely pick up a cross and follow Him.[5] You cannot begin to hope for revival until you willingly return to the very basics of what it means to be a Christian—the surrender of everything.[6]

True revival from God would be announced like this, "Come, everyone, give more of your money, goods, and self to the Lord." Not, "Come be blessed and gain your promise from the Lord." The last reveals Satanic selfishness,[7] while the other results from the joy that only the cross of Christ brings.

GOD'S TIMING

When revival happened the heads of fathers' households of Judah and Benjamin and the priests and the Levites arose, along with everyone whose spirit God had stirred to go up and rebuild the house of the Lord in Jerusalem. And all those about them encouraged them with articles of silver, with gold, with goods, with cattle, and with valuables, aside from all that was given as a freewill offering.

> Revival is marked by the absence of programs to gain money for the church.

God can "stir" only a remnant to "rebuild" the Christianity that they've lost. Revival always starts this way—as the calling of God and not as the schedule of man. Anyone who can schedule a revival on a certain date cannot be speaking by the Spirit of God. In the first place, revival does not happen in one day, but takes years to accomplish. Secondly, God does the stirring in the hearts of the people and does not use human effort[8] and the programs of man.

Revival is marked by the absence of programs to gain money for the church. As it was in the first church, so it is true with revival today. Those in the first church gave all, without outward prompting, and so everyone felt "encouraged" in the Lord. These people who "encourage" the work of the Lord with revival fire in their hearts cost Ananias and Sapphiria their lives. Ananias and Sapphira mocked the things of the Lord by not fully giving up all of self.[9] In Ezra 1:6 we read they "encouraged" the work; so too in Acts 4:36 we read that Barnabas means "Son of Encouragement." Why was he an encouragement?

> Now Joseph, a Levite of Cyprian birth, who was also called Barnabas by the apostles (which translated means, Son of Encouragement), and who owned a tract of land, sold it and brought the money and laid it at the apostles' feet. (Acts 4:36-37 NASB)

Now a man named Ananias, together with his wife Sapphira, also sold a piece of property. With his wife's full knowledge he kept back part of the money for himself, but brought the rest and put it at the apostles' feet. Then Peter said, "Ananias, how is it that Satan has so filled your heart that you have lied to the Holy Spirit and have kept for yourself some of the money you received for the land? Didn't it belong to you before it was sold? And after it was sold, wasn't the money at your disposal? What made you think of doing such a thing? You have not lied to men but to God." When Ananias heard this, he fell down and died. And great fear seized all who heard what had happened. (Acts 5:1-5)

The first church did not encourage the people to come to a revival with advertising hype and gimmicks to get something from God. The first church did not sell revival trinkets, nor were they interested in a numbers game. Instead, true revival came with a call to sacrifice all. Each person did not say to God, "Bless me," but rather, "Here God, we bless you."

> The first rewards of revival start after the people begin to surrender all, . . .

A people in whom God can stir up self-sacrifice and hatred[10] of their own lives, will once again find the treasures of the Lord they lost. They are ready for revival because they feel weary of self and all of their selfishness ways. Therefore, they respond to God's Spirit to sacrifice with joy. They consider it no cost to them, for the cost brought them untold joy.[11]

TREASURES FOUND AGAIN

The first rewards of revival start after the people begin to surrender all, so God allows them to discover some of His treasures again. The people in such revival get to taste a small sample of His joy and peace that is to come. The blessings, safely hidden away until their hearts softened again, are now brought out in the open. Although this revival represents a small sample of what is to come, it is rich by man's estimation. God's poverty more than equals all the riches of man. These first blessings that are brought out bless the Lord's house, not the people. God will always honor those who seek Him with this kind of selfless love. For their personal blessing is not to be blessed, but to bless the Lord.

> Also King Cyrus brought out the articles of the house of the Lord, which Nebuchadnezzar had carried away from Jerusalem and put in the house of his gods; and Cyrus, king of Persia, had them brought out by the hand of Mithredath the treasurer, and he counted them out to Sheshbazzar, the prince of Judah. Now this was their number: 30 gold dishes, 1,000 silver dishes, 29 duplicates; 30 gold bowls, 410 silver bowls of a second kind, and 1,000 other articles. All the articles of gold and silver numbered 5,400. Sheshbazzar brought them all up with the exiles who went up from Babylon to Jerusalem. (Ezra 1:7-11 NASB)

What a treasure even the small things of God are—"30 gold dishes," "1,000 silver dishes" and more. When revival begins in your life, don't rest with the small things the Lord begins to restore. Sacrifice and surrender daily, and richer treasures will be yours. Keep in "step with the Spirit" and you will have more of the Lord than you can begin to imagine.[12]

Revival doesn't have to be advertised. Everyone can see and feel it. When treasures are brought out, there is no need to tell everyone, "I am having a revival in my life." They will see the treasures themselves in quick order. In fact, if you have to convince anyone you are having a revival in your life, then you are not truly having one. This is why scripture says we should not love with "words," but in "action" and "truth."[13] If I had a dime for every Christian that said, "I love you. I will stand with you in the Lord," I would be a very wealthy man indeed! No one can hide a life radically changed and enriched by God's treasures.[14]

> How sad that those who need revival the most cling to their little acts of righteousness and thus forfeit these treasures.

How sad that those who need revival the most cling to their little acts of righteousness and thus forfeit these treasures. For them the words of Jesus will come true. Even what they "think they have" will be taken from them.[15] For all their boasting that they "need God" is nothing more than false humility. A false humility that tries to regain the first love they once had in the Lord, but on *their terms*. I know many who still wait to see if God will change the conditions of His gospel. They keep checking back in with me to see if something has changed.

God, however, will never bless false humility nor half confessions of sin. Such individuals who refuse to admit their hopelessness,[16] specifically confessing their sins,[17] will never experience revival. They will forever forfeit the treasures hidden in God's house because they want to come back to God on their terms.[18]

Those Returning

Revival by the power of the Spirit brings confession of failure and acknowledges disobedience to scripture. True revival admits dryness and its desperation for renewal in the Lord. People who admit their desperate need to repent stand ready for revival. Those who make the steps to return to a new calling of the Lord will be remembered by Him. Let us then read the following verse with reverence and awe. This is not some dry genealogical list of families, but the remnant willing to repent again. These families declared that they would return to the Lord with sacrifice. Let us read it as if our names were written down because we returned to the Lord. Read the list as if we hoped we would return with those who once knew the Lord.

Now these are the people of the province who came up out of the captivity of the exiles whom Nebuchadnezzar the king of Babylon had carried away to Babylon, and returned to Jerusalem and Judah, each to his city. These came with Zerubbabel, Jeshua, Nehemiah, Seraiah, Reelaiah, Mordecai, Bilshan, Mispar, Bigvai, Rehum, and Baanah. The number of the men of the people of Israel: the sons of Parosh, 2,172; the sons of Shephatiah, 372; the sons of Arah, 775; the sons of Pahath-moab of the sons of Jeshua and Joab, 2,812; the sons of Elam, 1,254; the sons of Zattu, 945; the sons of Zaccai, 760; the sons of Bani, 642; the sons of Bebai, 623; the sons of Azgad, 1,222; the sons of Adonikam, 666; the sons of Bigvai, 2,056; the sons of Adin, 454; the sons of Ater of Hezekiah, 98; the sons of Bezai, 323; the sons of Jorah, 112; the sons of Hashum, 223; the sons of Gibbar, 95; the men of Bethlehem, 123; the men of Netophah, 56; the men of Anathoth, 128; the sons of Azmaveth,

42; the sons of Kiriath-arim, Chephirah, and Beeroth, 743; the sons of Ramah and Geba, 621; the men of Michmas, 122; the men of Bethel and Ai, 223; the sons of Nebo, 52; the sons of Magbish, 156; the sons of the other Elam, 1,254; the sons of Harim, 320; the sons of Lod, Hadid, and Ono, 725; the men of Jericho, 345; the sons of Senaah, 3,630. The priests: the sons of Jedaiah of the house of Jeshua, 973; the sons of Immer, 1,052; the sons of Pashhur, 1,247; the sons of Harim, 1,017. The Levites: the sons of Jeshua and Kadmiel, of the sons of Hodaviah, 74. The singers: the sons of Asaph, 128. The sons of the gatekeepers: the sons of Shallum, the sons of Ater, the sons of Talmon, the sons of Akkub, the sons of Hatita, the sons of Shobai, in all 139. The temple servants: the sons of Ziha, the sons of Hasupha, the sons of Tabbaoth, the sons of Keros, the sons of Siaha, the sons of Padon, the sons of Lebanah, the sons of Hagabah, the sons of Akkub, the sons of Hagab, the sons of Shalmai, the sons of Hanan, the sons of Giddel, the sons of Gahar, the sons of Reaiah, the sons of Rezin, the sons of Nekoda, the sons of Gazzam, the sons of Uzza, the sons of Paseah, the sons of Besai, the sons of Asnah, the sons of Meunim, the sons of Nephisim, the sons of Bakbuk, the sons of Hakupha, the sons of Harhur, the sons of Bazluth, the sons of Mehida, the sons of Harsha, the sons of Barkos, the sons of Sisera, the sons of Temah, the sons of Neziah, the sons of Hatipha. The sons of Solomon's servants: the sons of Sotai, the sons of Hassophereth, the sons of Peruda, the sons of Jaalah, the sons of Darkon, the sons of Giddel, the sons of Shephatiah, the sons of Hattil, the sons of Pochereth-hazzebaim, the sons of Ami. All the temple servants, and the sons of Solomon's servants, were 392. Now these are those who came up from Tel-melah, Tel-harsha, Cherub, Addan, and Immer, but they were not able to give evidence of their fathers' households, and their descendants, whether they were of Israel: the sons of Delaiah, the sons of Tobiah, the sons of Nekoda, 652. (Ezra 2:1-60)

No Evidence

Before we press on, did you notice the end of the passage: ". . . but they were not able to give evidence of their father's households, and their descendants, whether they were of Israel . . ."? As revival begins some of the remnant will not even be allowed to try to repent. These are those who have passed the point of no return. They have lost their salvation. There is no evidence of the Spirit left and no tiny flicker that any amount of salvation is theirs in Christ. They had so little regard for the Lord and the blood that once sanctified them, that God will not let them return. Those in the Spirit can discern those who cannot give proof that they are "descendants" of Jesus. Those without proof of their ancestry remain doomed forever and should not be allowed to try to experience revival. They are those John declared we cannot pray for.[19] They are the sons and daughters of Hebrews for whom it is "impossible" to come back to God. How sad that I already know some people in this position.

> As revival begins some of the remnant will not even be allowed to try to repent. These are those who have passed the point of no return. They have lost their salvation.

> It is impossible for those who have once been enlightened, who have tasted the heavenly gift, who have shared in the Holy Spirit, who have tasted the goodness of the word of God and the powers of the coming age, if they fall away, to be brought back to repentance, because to their loss they are crucifying the Son of God all over again and subjecting him to public disgrace. (Heb. 6:4-6)

These are the type that no matter how many tears they shed in a revival, the blessing of reconciliation with God will not be given.[20]

Ezra shows us the good news of revival. There is no shortage of workers in this revival. Where once multitudes of workers labored for the Lord in hypocrisy, a few returned to the work in purity. Now there are workers, singers, builders, and laborers, when in the past it would have been hard to find volunteers. How many churches remain spiritually corrupted even now. The fact that they can't even find volunteers who are dead to self demonstrates this in these churches. In fact, the volunteers must have their flesh stroked or they will not work.

Yes, let us read their names with tears flowing down our checks. They returned to the Lord without any thought of self justification or getting anything from God; they are ready to be broken.

REMOVED

Revival certainly marks the regaining of what we lost, but it also denotes the losing of what we thought we possessed. The good we thought we did in the Lord is thrown out. We will hate and abhor the self-motivated worship and service to Jesus, because we cannot verify that it comes from God. Not to mention that we had sown good seed among weeds and so all our works were defiled.[22] We had "muddied" the waters for others who were trying to drink of the Lord's water and hindered others from worshipping the Lord in purity.[23]

A true revival "searches" to see what things, persons, and actions we have which do not come by the power of God. We put on hold those things that we cannot discern are of Him until He makes clear His will. Because of our hardness of heart and separation from God, we must wait for deeper revelations to reveal the right and wrong in the Lord on certain matters.[22]

And of the sons of the priests: the sons of Habaiah, the sons of Hakkoz, the sons of Barzillai, who took a wife from the daughters of Barzillai the Gileadite, and he was called by their name. These searched among their ancestral registration, but they could not be located; therefore they were considered unclean and excluded from the priesthood. And the governor said to them that they should not eat from the most holy things until a priest stood up with Urim and Thummim. (Ezra 2:61-63 NASB)

Even the "governor" noticed that some could not prove their spirituality and approval by God to do that work they once had done. Although they could be counted as worshippers, they would never be permitted to eat of the "holy things" of God. They were counted as "unclean," and not allowed to serve in the "priesthood," unless God made things clear at a later time by way of the "Urim and Thummim." There are some who, though still in the Lord, will never be permitted to do the work they once performed in the Lord. They will never be allowed to fulfill the high calling, the first call of God in their life. To the praise of God, though He shows them mercy, there will always be a dark cloud hanging over their lives. For they will know that the work of God is hindered and that they cannot be permitted to serve the Lord in that way again. Although saved by mercy, their stubbornness causes them to forfeit some blessings of God. Let them not take such discipline lightly, for fear they might lose something of greater value than work.

This forfeiture came from their lack of regard for Jesus.[24] They did not keep track of their "ancestral registration." When they had gone into captivity or the desert, they had tossed aside the precious thing God had given them. They did not guard their post when the king was angry.[25] They did not continue on in the work the Lord had given them. They thought they were being disciplined, so why bother. They acted like spoiled children who, if they can't have their way, will do very little required of them.

> Do not be "hasty" to say anything about God, scripture or right and wrong, until the cross has put some things to death in your life.

Very often those experiencing revival in the Lord feel that they all at once stood on firm ground. As a result, they will voice their thoughts and opinions about God and right and wrong in an instant. Let them be warned that they will have to wait until they find a priest to stand with the "Urim and Thummim." This is the way revival should happen. God sent the Israelites into captivity because they would not listen to their teachers, leaders, and prophets. It was like it is today, when most will not listen to any correction from teachers and will only gather around them teachers who will say what they want to hear. Many have the attitude that they don't need teachers. Even though they flatter their teachers, they actually believe they don't need them. They refuse the "gifts"[26] God sends and seek to find their own gifts. We will see if at the end of this revival the people will listen to their teachers.

Until the things that reveal God's will are present in your life, you must be silent.[27] In the deepest of humility, remember that you have fallen into a state where you need revival. So shut up and listen to God. Do not be "hasty" to say anything about God, scripture or right and wrong, until the cross has put some things to death in your life. "Guard your steps" carefully.

REVIVAL BEGINS • 61

Guard your steps as you go to the house of God, and draw near to listen rather than to offer the sacrifice of fools; for they do not know they are doing evil. Do not be hasty in word or impulsive in thought to bring up a matter in the presence of God. For God is in heaven and you are on the earth; therefore let your words be few. (Ecc. 5:1-2)

"Impulsive" is the only way to describe those who had to be sent into captivity and those just returning from captivity. They immediately sanction any religious impulse as being "of the Lord." Those often getting ready to go into captivity will speak excessively in the name of the Lord. Since they justify every whim of the flesh, they act and speak as if the Lord told them to act upon the impulse. Therefore, Jeremiah told the people, as God prepared to send them into captivity, that they must not say, "The Lord told me." Just before captivity, the people in Jeremiah's day seemed so eager to know God's will. They would come to the prophet and ask, "What is the Lord's answer to you?" and "What has the Lord spoken?" God said that because of this duplicity, He would "cast you out of my presence, . . . forget you, and bring upon you everlasting disgrace—everlasting shame."

This is what each of you keeps on saying to his friend or relative: "What is the Lord's answer?" or "What has the Lord spoken?" But you must not mention "the oracle of the Lord" again, because every man's own word becomes his oracle and so you distort the words of the living God, the Lord Almighty, our God. This is what you keep saying to a prophet: "What is the Lord's answer to you?" or "What has the Lord spoken?" Although you claim, "This is the oracle of the Lord," this is what the Lord says: You used the words, "This is the oracle of the Lord," even though

I told you that you must not claim, "This is the oracle of the Lord." Therefore, I will surely forget you and cast you out of my presence along with the city I gave to you and your fathers. I will bring upon you everlasting disgrace—everlasting shame that will not be forgotten. (Jer. 23:35-40)

> If God calls you back by way of revival, then know this: He will powerfully seek to shut you up.

Those on the verge of captivity quickly chat about the Lord. Phrases sputter from their lips like: "What did the Lord show you?"…"What do feel God has told you?"…"The Lord has shown me this."…"The Lord is really working!"…"What has God shown you about the scripture?"

They do this for two reasons. First, they feel guilt about where they are at in the Lord and seek to buy time by appearing to be obedient. Secondly, their own desires have replaced the Lord's voice, and so they feel that the Lord is in what they want.

The cause of this can be found in Jeremiah 23:36. They take their own thoughts, impulses, and desires and tack on the name of the Lord—"because every man's own word becomes his oracle and so you distort the words of the living God." They transform their thoughts into the will of God. Such people reject the cross that would have crucified those impulses. They have no discernment left as to God's will because they will not let the cross do its testing work.[28] The mix between their lies and God's truth has become so polluted that discernment as to God's will is impossible.

If God calls you back by way of revival, then know this: He will powerfully seek to shut you up. Every thought, every action, every understanding of scripture, every work, every prayer, every sharing of the gospel, and every religious impulse must be tested by the cross of Christ. If revival happens, then sit down and close your mouth.[29] If this is God's advice to the young in the Lord, how much more should those starting over listen? Do as the passage below says: "sit alone and be silent."

> It is good for a man that he should bear the yoke in his youth. Let him sit alone and be silent since He has laid it on him. Let him put his mouth in the dust; perhaps there is hope. Let him give his cheek to the smiter; let him be filled with reproach. For the Lord will not reject forever, for if He causes grief, then He will have compassion according to His abundant loving-kindness. (Lam. 3:27-32 NASB)

Therefore, go and obey this passage. Go put "dust" in your mouth and see how much talking you can do. People returning from discipline talk so much because they are still unsettled in their spirits. They desperately want to be right with the Lord, to hear His voice again, and to feel the Holy Spirit's presence. But as we have seen, revival takes time. Advise them to go sit down in the dust; invite rebukes from God's Word and godly men while they meditate on the "abundant loving-kindness" of God. For the kindness of God often comes out in rebukes.[30] Indeed, if you are returning to the Lord, it is a privilege that God would try rebuking you again. If your church is in revival, then it is a great kindness that God would take the time to rebuke you.

Advise those returning, to "be filled" with "reproach" and let God deal with the sin that sent them into captivity in the first place. If they will do this, they will find that God does "not reject forever" and they will find the "compassion" they so long for. If those returning to the Lord are unwilling to do this, then they are unworthy of your time[31] or the Lord's revival.

Whatever you believe about this, know for certain one thing. Whenever someone who is around you talks excessively, or who has story after story, sin is present in their lives.

> When words are many, sin is not absent, but he who holds his tongue is wise. (Prov. 10:19)

PAUSE

Scripture pauses again to note those who sacrifice unto the Lord, and so shall we pause. We repeat many matters in this book because God repeats them. If the Lord desires to point something out again in scripture, then let us break the rules of writing and repeat it.[32]

> **How sad that most church services in the name of Jesus are actually "idolatry." They just try to get something from Jesus and will not let Him crucify them.**

Some of the heads of fathers' households, when they arrived at the house of the Lord which is in Jerusalem, offered willingly for the house of God to restore it on its foundation. According to their ability they gave to the treasury for the work 61,000 gold drachmas, and 5,000 silver minas, and 100 priestly garments. (Ezra 2:68-69 NASB)

God pauses to remind us of this one thing. Sacrifice begins revival, flames revival, and sustains revival. So many wait and pray for revival when God has already tried to answer those prayers. But they put out the flames because they, and the people they pray for, refuse to sacrifice self and doctrines. As the passage above shows, sacrifice lays the "foundation" of revival. A sacrifice "willingly" motivated, without prompting from men in any way, opens the way for revival. We are talking about sacrifice of self, not just money. How many people will stand before God and say, "But we prayed for revival," only to hear God say, "But I did try to answer; you just refused to respond"?

The truly repentant will not sacrifice to get something from God. That is the beginning of idol worship. You lay your gift at the altar to be blessed and to ward off evil. However, God warns Christians. . .

Therefore, my beloved, flee from idolatry. (1 Cor. 10:14 NASB)

How sad that most church services in the name of Jesus are actually "idolatry." They just try to get something from Jesus and will not let Him crucify them. This is why rebellion[33] is like witch-craft or divination. Those in rebellion think that if they get the doctrine correct and the words just right, it will cause God to move in their favor. Just as a witch believes that if she gets the words correct, the spirits will obey her.

However, those who love God have given up all pretense to their righteousness. They no longer say, "I am thankful God doesn't show me all of my sin at once." They now see that they must let God come to them in any way He sees fit, in His timing. In fact, they "hunger and thirst for righteousness"[34] so much that they wish God would show them all their sins at once. This is how Isaiah, Job, and others were blessed, and it is the only way we too will be blessed.[35]

My ears had heard of you but now my eyes have seen you. There-fore I despise myself and repent in dust and ashes. (Job 42:5-6)

UNITY

Seven months later, in the book of Ezra, the people gather to continue God's revival. A halting of worship activity occurs between each pause of revival. They had to halt at certain points and not move further into worship because the Holy Spirit stopped them. As each continued to do his part, they were limited in the depth to which they could go into worship. God had to prepare certain things and ready their hearts for the next step into revival. He prepared them for Himself – the goal of revival. The same remains for those who experience revival today. God takes away our worship and songs that we might worship in Spirit and Truth.

> Take away from Me the noise of your songs; I will not even listen to the sound of your harps. (Amos 5:23 NASB)

God's Spirit moves the people into worship and work but must stop until everything is ready for the next stage. Just as a woman's body prepares itself with labor pains, so does the pause prepare for revival. The stopping and starting of labor pains allow the body to adjust and the baby to get into a better position for birth. In the same way, pausing in revival allows God to cleanse more sin, to instruct us in the Word, to place more of His Spirit in us, and to prepare us for the next step toward God's holy mountain. If the labor went on constantly, it would

> Don't be surprised if your church experiences revival, that God stops all activity, or at least slows things way down for months at a time.

kill the baby and the mother. Likewise, God pauses to allow us to adjust to the pains of revival.

Don't be surprised if your church experiences revival, that God stops all activity, or at least slows things way down for months at a time. You must be taught to wait upon God and not do as you did in the past,[36] when you acted for and on behalf of God rather than letting His Spirit do the work in you. Remember Saul and how he did not wait for the Lord![37]

God must also work unity between you and Him and between you and your brothers and sisters for revival to finish its work. Revival without this goal is a revival of selfishness that makes one "twice" as fit for hell.[38]

While those questionable things in the Lord must wait for the "Urim," the Lord works real unity by the Spirit. This is not a man-made compromise where everyone "agrees to disagree," but a unity where everyone begins to think the same thoughts because the cross is crucifying their minds and giving them the mind of Christ. The Israelites had grown weary and were willing to die to their thoughts, motives, church doctrines, and wisdom. This allowed the Spirit to work a little more of His thoughts[39] into each and every person. At each stage of revival we see the creation of "one man" in the Lord.

> Now when the seventh month came, and the sons of Israel were in the cities, the people gathered together as one man to Jerusalem. (Ezra 3:1 NASB)

This verse emphasizes "as one man." As each man hates his own thoughts, he gladly accepts God's thoughts and this brings men into unity.[40] Is this not what the New Testament is all about? Is this not what we are commanded to be in Christ?

Now I exhort you, brethren, by the name of our Lord Jesus Christ, that you all agree, and there be no divisions among you, but you be made complete in the same mind and in the same judgment. (1 Cor. 1:10 NASB)

Do you see what this passage states? It says that "you be made complete" in Christ. How are we made "complete"? By allowing God to do His work of unity in us. Look at the first church after the revival started on the day of Pentecost. The Bible says they "were of one heart and soul." Is it little wonder that the apostles could testify about the Lord with "great power" and that "abundant grace was upon them all"? They were in unity.

And the congregation of those who believed were of one heart and soul; and not one of them claimed that anything belonging to him was his own; but all things were common property to them. And with great power the apostles were giving witness to the resurrection of the Lord Jesus, and abundant grace was upon them all. (Acts 4:32-33 NASB)

Again we see the sacrifice of worldly goods ("all things were common property") and the unity of thought ("of one heart and soul") that accompanies revival. If a church claims revival and you do not see these two simple things, they live a lie. Unless you see this perfect unity and sacrifice in your church, revival is not happening.

A FOUNDATION OF SACRIFICE

Then Jeshua son of Jozadak and his fellow priests and Zerubbabel son of Shealtiel and his associates began to build the altar of the God of Israel to sacrifice burnt offerings on it, in accordance with what is written in the Law of Moses the man of God. Despite their fear of the peoples around them, they built the altar on its foundation and sacrificed burnt offerings on it to the Lord, both the morning and evening sacrifices. Then in accordance with what is written, they celebrated the Feast of Tabernacles with the *required* number of burnt offerings prescribed for each day. After that, they presented the regular burnt offerings, the New Moon sacrifices and the sacrifices for all the appointed sacred feasts of the Lord, as well as those brought as freewill offerings to the Lord. (Ezra 3:2-5, emphasis added)

> The Israelite people had stopped obeying, just as many have stopped doing the simple things required from Jesus—the prayer times, holding your tongue, despising money, loving people, being disciplined with the TV, radio, music (even Christian), computer, sports and more.

As we move through the chapters of Ezra, we see the revival winds gathering force. Revival begins to work the traditional and daily acts of worship in the people. At this point, the people begin to do the things "required" of them. However, this was not yet deep fellowship with the Lord. How sad that many count daily sacrifice as their supreme offerings and work in the Lord. Such individuals are not true lovers of God, but try to manipulate God into giving them salvation. They expect to do the things required of everyone and be rewarded with a prophet's reward. These individuals always have an exaggerated opinion of their walk with God.

The required things of Jesus consist of what any child knows should be done in the Lord. They include the simple things that we know God will help us accomplish. God expects anyone who claims to be a Christian to understand and fulfill the "daily" acts of obedience. The Israelite people had stopped obeying, just as many have stopped doing the simple things required from Jesus—the prayer times, holding our tongues, despising money, loving people,[41] keeping Sunday holy, being disciplined with the TV, radio, music (even Christian),[42] computer, sports and more.

The Israelites had grown spiritually to the point that they performed the daily "required number" of righteous things again. In fact, the people had even grown a little beyond that point and obeyed the Lord in deeper affairs. Remember that "freewill offerings" and sacrifices permeated all the people's obedience. They served the Lord with joy. They willingly denied themselves in anyway they could so that the Holy Spirit could come along with some really important matters of denying self. In short, if you had "judged" yourself, you would not have fallen under "judgment."[43] If you would have "beaten" your body to make it "your slave," you would not have been sent into captivity. If you would have obeyed the rules of the race, you would not have been taken out of the race. Christians must obey these simple basic things. The Jews obeyed without being told to and began to put their lives in order.

I do all this for the sake of the gospel, that I may share in its blessings. Do you not know that in a race all the runners run, but only one gets the prize? Run in such a way as to get the prize. Everyone who competes in the games goes into strict training. They do it to get a crown that will not last; but we do it to get a crown that will last forever. Therefore I do not run like a man running aimlessly; I do not fight like a man beating the air. No, I beat my body and make it my slave so that after I have preached to others, I myself will not be disqualified for the prize. (1 Cor. 9:23-27)

Do you want to "share in" the "blessings" of the gospel? Then you must begin to "run in such as way to get the prize," go into "strict training," do not "run aimlessly," do not "beat the air," rather make your body obey you. Sit down right now and make a list of the goals you

> Like little pigs, they selfishly get what they want from the Lord and sit back to wallow in the mud.

know the Lord has for you that will cause you to deny self. Then write down the "rules" that you must apply to yourself to get there. Lay the foundation of sacrifice and God will meet you there to guide and direct. Lay the foundation for denial of self, hating your life, and get your life in order. Become empowered with the basic things in Christ and you shall be led to drink deeper of the cup of crucifixion.[44] Good news? Only to those who love God.

Above all, revival returns to sacrifice. The revival in the book of Ezra moved the people to sacrifice more to the Lord. They had remained obedient to the Lord with purity of heart at the beginning stirrings of the Holy Spirit and now were permitted to lay the "foundation" for daily sacrifice.

Many who have fallen into sin fail at this point. They see their need for revival, and as God begins to blow His revival winds, they sacrifice for awhile and then stop. The little bit of peace and freedom they gained back satisfies them. Like little pigs, they selfishly get what they want from the Lord and sit back to wallow in the mud.

Jesus answered them and said, "Truly, truly, I say to you, you seek Me, not because you saw signs, but because you ate of the loaves, and were filled." (John 6:26 NASB)

How many show up at meetings only to get their blessing? Indeed, false meetings advertise revival that way. Not true for these Israelites. Since those in Ezra's day fell in love with God again, the Lord permitted them to lay the "foundation" for daily sacrifice. They resolved never again to be found lacking in sacrificing to the Lord. Never again would they need revival, because they would always joyfully and "daily" carry their crosses.

Then he said to them all: "If anyone would come after me, he must deny himself and take up his cross daily and follow me." (Luke 9:23)

These people were renewed in giving everything to God, every hour of every day. They sacrificed "each day's" requirements along with "burnt offerings" and a "continual burnt offering." They sacrificed to God every thought, every act, and everything about themselves. When they got up, what they read, whom they talked to, when they ate lunch—was all given over to the Lord.

This is our assurance of salvation, the continual growing sacrifice of ourselves. The people of Israel did this by celebrating the "Feast of Booths." Each family built a booth and began sacrificing at their homes in the wilderness. Revival began with each household realizing they are not of this world and setting themselves in order. A revival that does not start quietly at home and move toward the church as a whole is not of the Lord. This explains why large gatherings of people for revival never last. God's revival begins in each heart and moves out among the people. Anything else demonstrates nothing more than the hype you see at a sports event. One creates man's revival, while the other responds to the Spirit's call.

Ezra 3:6 tells us that sacrifice began before the temple was built. This teaches that revival is not the taking up of a church building fund. Revival is not the paving of the church parking lot.

> From the first day of the seventh month they began to offer burnt offerings to the Lord, but the foundation of the temple of the Lord had not been laid. (Ezra 3:6 NASB)

The reason for this is crystal clear. Any church that is building a structure for worship gains a certain amount of natural unity and revival. Even the world finds this to be true. This is nothing more than a natural revival that results from human effort and zeal devoted to a project, even with the repentance that may result from it.

> Why do you think churches always advertise that they have "exciting" worship services? They know how easily people become bored and that this will pull away members from other churches.

Many ministries fall prey to this kind of revival, since churches easily unite for a cause. Then, when the building is finished, the church begins to have troubles again. In fact, this is why pastors are taught to keep one new project going after another. Otherwise, boredom would set in, the flock would grumble and the pastor might lose his job. Why do you think churches always advertise that they have "exciting" worship services? They know how easily people become bored and that this will pull away members from other churches. This is why song leaders always must tell the congregation, "We feel the presence of God." They must keep the sheep content and entertained.

One reason God must pause when bringing revival is that it is too easy for men to worship the revival more than Him who causes the revival. Each man is tested by how he responds to these interludes of boredom. Does he need the excitement of the world—the business of the world, miracles, revival fires—or is God enough?

> But anyone who labors for God without a foundation of sacrificing pride, self-will, self-centeredness, and self-determination is not moved by God.

Such causes give a false sense of purpose, work, and love for God. We think that because we become involved in a good cause, God must love us, and we feel close to Him. This is the great temptation for those who work in front-line ministries and causes. If you have that kind of position, remember well that you could be "disqualified for the prize" no matter how noble the ministry.[45]

But anyone who labors for God without a foundation of sacrificing pride, self-will, self-centeredness, and self-determination is not moved by God. Oh, they might be used by God, but they are not truly in God. The sacrifice of the self that lives in our hearts must begin first before we ever lay the foundation for the temple. Lay self on the altar fire before we ever participate in a work men can see outwardly; let the aroma of death to self be what everyone smells first. Let no man join your work or church until this foundation has been laid. Not to do so shows God that you love your works more than His righteousness and have no real love for those who labor with you.[46]

Four things must be present to know God's will, and your workers must give themselves to them. For those returning from captivity or the desert, these things represent the "Urim and Thumimim." These things must be worked in them before they can talk of God's will. The four things are found in the passage below. They are:

1. View God's Mercy.
2. Offer Your Body.
3. Do Not Conform.
4. Be Transformed.

Therefore, I urge you, brothers, in view of God's mercy, to offer your bodies as living sacrifices, holy and pleasing to God—this is your spiritual act of worship. Do not conform any longer to the pattern of this world, but be transformed by the renewing of your mind. Then you will be able to test and approve what God's will is—his good, pleasing and perfect will. (Rom. 12:1-2)

(1) The humility must be present, (2) they must offer up all of self unto the Lord in very specific ways, (3) they reject the way of the world, (4) they will let the Holy Spirit remold their minds. When all of this is present in large measures, then and *only then* can they "test" and "approve" what is God's will. How many think they can hear God's voice when not even half these things are present!

Read, and then read again Ezra 3:2-5. The priests had become the example of self-sacrifice. They returned to obeying God's word and began to worship again in the way the Lord had told all men to worship Him. No more women preachers, no more begging for money, no more uncovered women, no more divorce and then remarriage, no singles groups, no greed, and more. In short, hypocrisy from the pulpit would be put to an end. Such men would be called "legalistic" in today's hostile spiritual climate of the church.

Strength To Strength

Do you see the stages of true revival so far? First the quiet call to start sacrificing again to the Lord begins. Then a pause in worship while each rebuilds the things God has revealed so far in his life. Then, when God designates the appropriate time, the foundation for daily sacrifice is laid. At each stage, the people deal with a little more sin and they experience a little more repentance and joy. This should be true for God's people throughout their whole Christian life, but in revival times this intensifies.

> They go from strength to strength, till each appears before God in Zion. (Ps. 84:7)

When a Christian stops going from "strength to strength," then only revival can restore this normal condition.

Permission

God gave permission, through the king of Persia, for revival to begin and reminds us of this in the next verse. Let us also take double warning.

Here we are again back at the "permission" of God. Most individuals and churches do not wait for "permission" from God for revival. Like the noisy crowd of sinners, they lay claim to revival as if it were their right.[47] They advertise revival, claim God gives them revival and refuse to wait upon God to move others to revival. Instead, they invite whomever they want to come to their church revival. They worship numbers and think that high attendance denotes revival. They motivate others with all manner of schemes and programs to attend their revival meetings. But the people in Ezra's day knew that revival should only happen by God's permission, not of their desire. They dare not sin by giving to the work of revival if God has not granted permission to do so. So many falsely believe that they can return to God

> Most individuals and churches do not wait for "permission" from God for revival. Like the noisy crowd of sinners, they lay claim to revival as if it were their right.

when they choose to. It is never a question of whether they want to return to God, but whether God will accept them back or not.[48]

> Then they gave money to the masons and carpenters, and food, drink, and oil to the Sidonians and to the Tyrians, to bring cedar wood from Lebanon to the sea at Joppa, according to the permission they had from Cyrus king of Persia. (Ezra 3:7 NASB)

They had "permission" by the "king of Persia" for this revival. This revival began in God's timing and in God's way.[49] There was no hype involved, only the quiet moving of the Holy Spirit. These people stayed solemn in spirit because they felt extremely fortunate that God had given "permission" for revival through the king. These people did not presumptuously[50] march in to take the promised land. There were no worldly revival preachers among them who advertised themselves.[51] They did not apply the principles of revival to their lives and only read the foolish how-to books on revival. These people were holy, waiting in quietness for God to act. These individuals waited upon God with fear and trembling before doing anything.[52] After all, revival returns the people to doing God's will, and they resolve not to miss God's will in this issue called revival.

CHAPTER SIX

IN THE MIDST
OF REVIVAL

R EVIVAL DOES NOT HAPPEN IN A WEEKEND OR A DAY. THOSE IN NEED
of revival require years of repentance. If you have sinned to
the point that you need revival, do not think for an instant that you
will be built up and renewed in a weekend. It takes years to undo that
which you have destroyed in the Lord by your stubbornness and sin.

There is only one way to know if revival takes hold of your life
over the years. Look at what denial to self you allow the Holy Spirit
to increase in your life every day. (See the passage below.) The Israelites were in the second year of revival . . . certainly no weekend
pumped up event.

> Now in the second year of their coming to the house of God at
> Jerusalem in the second month, Zerubbabel the son of Shealtiel
> and Jeshua the son of Jozadak and the rest of their brothers the
> priests and the Levites, and all who came from the captivity to
> Jerusalem, began the work and appointed the Levites from twenty
> years and older to oversee the work of the house of the Lord.
> (Ezra 3:8 NASB)

Revival calls for hard work and those appointed must labor strongly and intensely. Revival does not stem from an emotional high that a revival preacher produces from a week-long preaching event at your church. Ezra 3:8 shows us that revival, or "the work of the Lord," didn't even begin until two years later. Revival causes also the appointment of men only who are worthy to work at repentance, whereas in the past, the people would have appointed anyone and accepted any volunteer.[1]

> Revival does not stem from an emotional high that a revival preacher produces from a week-long preaching event at your church.

Those who were eighteen years old when the foundation for the altar was laid had now turned twenty years old and were eligible for appointed work. For two years, these young men had prepared themselves for this day by daily sacrificing unto the Lord. How many fail at revival in their lives? God started to answer their prayers to revive them. However, two years later, when He was ready for the work to begin, many had returned to their old sins. They had not prepared themselves and gotten "ready" to do the work when God was quiet. They squandered their time on petty sins and worldly thoughts. They grew bored and restless and went off in "small" ways to please themselves.

> But suppose the servant says to himself, "My master is taking a long time in coming," and he then begins to beat the menservants and maidservants and to eat and drink and get drunk. The master of that servant will come on a day when he does not expect him and at an hour he is not aware of. He will cut him to pieces

and assign him a place with the unbelievers. That servant who knows his master's will and does not get ready or does not do what his master wants will be beaten with many blows. (Luke 12:45-47)

These people did not grow in death to self during those two years, but were content to indulge themselves in the Lord. During those bleak times, they did not grow in their knowledge of scriptures. They were busy and had no desire to be renewed according to the Word. They were more busy reading books about the Word, rather than drinking "pure spiritual milk."[2] They were bored with scripture and had to be entertained by "Christian" novels, plays, and cartoons. They wanted sermons that entertained rather than preached the Word.[3] They did not get the temple ready, make provision, practice their gift and/or get organized while in captivity.

If you are in need of revival, then just ask yourself the following: "Do I know scripture from ink[4] more than when I first went into captivity?" I say "ink," because the Spirit may not have been speaking to you,[5] but you should have at least stood at your post memorizing scripture. Those wandering in the desert should be able to quote scripture left and right – even though there is no life in them. If you haven't prepared yourself this way, why should God revive you?

I am exceedingly afflicted; Revive me, O Lord, according to Thy word. (Ps. 119:107 NASB)

God renews according to His Word only, and those who have continued to store that Word in their hearts will be far more ready for revival than those who have forgotten that Word. As a side note, a church where the members do not quote scriptures to each other on a daily basis desperately needs revival. For if there is one thing

Christians should be rich in, it is quoting scripture to each other by the direction of the Holy Spirit.

> Blessed are those who let revival do its work, for they will not only find an abundance of workers, but will have those who are qualified to "oversee" the work of the cross in others' lives.

Let the word of Christ dwell in you richly as you teach and admonish one another with all wisdom, and as you sing psalms, hymns and spiritual songs with gratitude in your hearts to God. (Col. 3:16)

Blessed are those who let revival do its work, for they will not only find an abundance of workers, but will have those who are qualified to "oversee" the work of the cross in others' lives.[6]

Then Jeshua with his sons and brothers stood united with Kadmiel and his sons, the sons of Judah and the sons of Henadad with their sons and brothers the Levites, to oversee the workmen in the temple of God. (Ezra 3:9 NASB)

True revival allows men to stand "united" in the Lord. Such men can labor together and show others how to labor, because each dies to his own opinion on matters. Where you find revival fire unity, you will find God giving "life forevermore."[7]

It takes at least two years before one can ever really pronounce that revival by God's Spirit has taken hold in someone's life. If after two years they have humbled themselves, allowed God's Word to work its daily work of sacrifice, then and only then can we speak of revival. Prior to this time they had only been making right the obvious wrongs in their lives. Up until this point, they had been living the baptism of John that prepares the way for the Lord to come to them at a later date.[8] Let everyone, just beginning to experience revival, give themselves over fully to the baptism of John. Then they will be ready for Jesus to come to them. To "reject" this baptism of John is to forfeit Jesus when He comes to you later.

> But the Pharisees and experts in the law rejected God's purpose for themselves, because they had not been baptized by John. (Luke 7:30)

> It takes at least two years before one can ever really pronounce that revival by God's Spirit has taken hold in someone's life.

The baptism of John is repentance in specific things in our lives. It is a baptism that says, "What can we do?"[9] so that Jesus can come to us with the Holy Spirit at a later time. A man who can order his life by asking, "What can I do?" will also ask the same question at Pentecost, "What shall we do?"[10] Those who ask this question and put forth real action will be given the Holy Spirit. Those who begin in self-effort to follow the Lord will be shown its futility and will receive the Holy Spirit. Those who whine that they do not want to act because they do not want to fall into "self-effort" are just giving excuses for being "wicked" and "lazy." Such individuals will be "thrown outside into the darkness."[11]

In other words, until this time the Jews had only sacrificed the self they could easily reason with and discern. Up until this time, they had been repenting only of what the preacher or prophets pointed out. The fire that only the Holy Spirit can bring had not taken place and wouldn't take place until the people were prepared. Like those at Pentecost, it would take three years of Jesus' preaching and dying on the cross to prepare them for that day.

Up until this time, their brokenness had been shallow compared to what God had prepared for them. Until now it had only been the preaching of John the Baptist, but it soon would be the fire of the Holy Spirit. How many refuse the Spirit's work at this point with self-righteous objections? They complain that they have already confessed their sins and cleaned up many things.[12] They insist that they have already wept and admitted their need for revival. They forgot that revival, like crucifixion and childbirth, is a slow process until the last final moments.[13]

These Jews had prepared themselves over the years for the Lord, and now God prepares to move in a stronger way. Remember, God will only give us our food at the "proper time," (Luke 12:42). So few have their sails set ready to catch the wind of the Lord when He begins to blow the Spirit again. How few have sails trimmed and ready even with no wind in sight. How few wait for the Lord rather than row to shore to indulge in self once again. The entire book of Ezra covers eighty years, and the waiting time between chapters six and seven lasted fifty years. God will hold back His Holy Spirit sometimes for years. Will we be found ready, sacrificing, working, and waiting when He does decide to move again?

Just look at what takes place after two years. The people had been obedient up to this point. They had proven themselves faithful enough for God to work more revival in their lives.[14] They were dressed in the correct "apparel" or good deeds for this level. They returned to following God's Word "to praise the Lord according to the directions of King David."

Now when the builders had laid the foundation of the temple of the Lord, the priests stood in their apparel with trumpets, and the Levites, the sons of Asaph, with cymbals, to praise the Lord according to the directions of King David of Israel. And they sang, praising and giving thanks to the Lord, saying, "For He is good, for His lovingkindness is upon Israel forever." And all the people shouted with a great shout when they praised the Lord because the foundation of the house of the Lord was laid. (Ezra 3:10-11 NASB)

How many will miss the "cymbals," "praise," and joy when revival does not come as quickly as they would like? The Israelites became faithless and lazy because God didn't move fast enough. How many said to themselves, "See, the prophets were wrong. God wasn't really with them," then sat back and smugly quit?

> How many will miss the "cymbals," "praise," and joy when revival does not come as quickly as they would like?

It took two full years just to get to a place where the foundation of the temple could be laid. It took that long for the obedience and spiritual purity to take place. Many find themselves running late when it comes to this matter called revival. They still do not get ready for the foundation of the church to be laid, because they continue working on the foundation for sacrifice! They still don't get dressed and ready for service. They still don't know the direction of God for their life even in the small things. Indeed, what small things they do see, they cannot be obedient to in the Spirit. Their hearts remain impure in motive and thought. They keep working on the issue of hating their own lives and denying self. Not only are they not ready for the temple work, they continue as infants in the Lord, crying for more milk. Those who still need milk in the Lord, years later, never changed from mere "babes" and are not fit to discuss righteousness in the Lord, let alone to share at Sunday School. Why do you think so many pastors preach primarily "salvation messages" at every worship service? Because their congregation loves milk and doesn't want to be required to do the righteous things of God.

> Concerning him we have much to say, and it is hard to explain, since you have become dull of hearing. For though by this time you ought to be teachers, you have need again for someone to teach you the elementary principles of the oracles of God, and you have come to need milk and not solid food. For everyone who partakes only of milk is not accustomed to the word of righteousness, for he is a babe. (Heb. 5:11-13 NASB)

Anyone who has been in the Lord for years and is not qualified to teach has some very serious problems. If, after all that time, they cannot teach others about the glories and the pain of the cross, then they are babes who may be sent into captivity. Hebrews 5:12 declares that if you can't teach about the crucified life by the example of your life, then you are not acquainted with righteousness; you have little if any wisdom to deal with others' problems. You cannot speak of God "powerfully" working His wisdom in you that can "perfect" others in Christ.[15] You are not familiar with what is holy in the Lord – no matter how much you share the gospel with others or speak of God working in your life.

Again, let me remind you that even the book of Hebrews says that we must have God's "permission" before we can move on to other things in the Lord. We must have permission from God to verify that we have matured before moving on. A baby is not born in a week and you will not regain lost ground in a month. Before you claim to move on to anything else in the Lord, make sure you have God's permission.

And God permitting, we will do so. (Heb. 6:3)

We must think of revival as permitted steps to renewal.[16] God responds to your sinful backsliding and begins to bring you back from captivity, but not in your timing. You tell God you want restoration in Him, so He takes you at your word. Then, step by step, He leads you toward reconciliation with Him. You can refuse, however, and go on in the same stubbornness that sent you into captivity in the first place—so watch your heart and life!

> We must think of revival as permitted steps to renewal.

Above all else, guard your heart, for it is the wellspring of life. (Prov. 4:23)

CHAPTER SEVEN

THE REVIVAL CRY

Yet many of the priests and Levites and heads of fathers' households, the old men who had seen the first temple, wept with a loud
voice when the foundation of this house was laid before their eyes,
while many shouted aloud for joy; so that the people could not
distinguish the sound of the shout of joy from the sound of the
weeping of the people, for the people shouted with a loud shout,
and the sound was heard far away. (Ezra 3:12-13 NASB)

WHAT A CRY! THE "HEADS OF FATHERS' HOUSEHOLDS" WEPT. "OLD
men" wept while many others shouted for "joy." What a
strange cry or sound went "far" out into the land. No one could tell
if the people were shouting for joy or weeping. Whoever heard this
cry knew it wasn't entertainment taking place. The priest did not
tell stories and crack jokes from the pulpit.[1] There is no sound like
that of a people in the mist of revival. It is an unearthly strange cry
not often heard. It is "loud" and prays just as Jesus prayed while on
earth.[2] Just as Jesus prayed and learned obedience from what He

suffered, you, even in revival, will be reconciled to God in the same way. The passage below is the revival cry lived out in Jesus.

> During the days of Jesus' life on earth, he offered up prayers and petitions with loud cries and tears to the one who could save him from death, and he was heard because of his reverent submission. Although he was a son, he learned obedience from what he suffered. (Heb. 5:7-8)

The next passage tells us the only way we too can overcome sin. As you "suffer in your body," a revival cry will be heard by everyone because God tries desperately to form Christ in you again. 1 Peter is straight forward. Only those prepared to "suffer" with this "attitude" will find victory over sin.

> Therefore, since Christ suffered in his body, arm yourselves also with the same attitude, because he who has suffered in his body is done with sin. As a result, he does not live the rest of his earthly life for evil human desires, but rather for the will of God. (1 Pet. 4:1-2)

This type of revival produces a sorrow and rejoicing that only the cross can work and magnify in intensity. It replicates the cry of Jesus as He nears the end of the crucifixion, "My God, My God! Why have you forsaken me?" Yet this cry mixes with the cry of faith, "Into your hands I commit my spirit." Every Christian should walk with this cry on their lips every day, but it intensifies during revival times.

> as sorrowful yet always rejoicing, . . . (2 Cor. 6:10 NASB)

This sorrow results from the cross working in each of us daily. The cry consists of the resurrected life that comes from death to self. We feel God's judgment of our sin and His mercy deep in our souls. No more self-pity that comes from conviction of sin. Gone too is the self-righteousness that refuses to weep over sin. If you do not hear this cry, you will not witness true revival. The rejoicing does not come from falsely claiming God's mercy, nor does it come from whining over sin. This cry happens in the Holy Spirit's timing and power; man cannot produce it. Man can mock it, but he cannot produce it. This cry rejoices in God's mercy and weeps at what was lost because of sin.

> If you do not hear this cry, you will not witness true revival.

When man experiences false revival, he either wants joy or sorrow, but not both. He wants to rejoice about God's mercy, ignoring his sin and correction. Or he wants to weep about his sins without repentance in his life, boasting of his false humility.

How few find weeping equal to rejoicing in the Lord. They clamor that those who do are too hard on themselves. Those refusing this joyful sorrow say we should just claim the blood of Jesus and move on. However, to those in the Spirit, weeping is the sound of joy, and the sound of joy is weeping.

Blessed are you who weep now, for you shall laugh. (Luke 6:21 NASB)

Let us not be fooled at this point. Revival might have taken a foothold, but they are not yet reconciled fully to the Lord. Foothold revival is not full revival, just as the beginnings of child birth does not mean the birth of a child. When someone finds revival, only the end of revival matters— reconciliation with God.

> The end of a matter is better than its beginning . . . (Ecc. 7:8)

Until we can, by the permission of the Holy Spirit, state that someone has been reconciled to God, we cannot say that revival has done its work. Why do you think God writes the following to Christians: that we should be "found at peace with him"?

> The Lord is not slow about His promise, as some count slowness, but is patient toward you, not wishing for any to perish but for all to come to repentance. But the day of the Lord will come like a thief, in which the heavens will pass away with a roar and the elements will be destroyed with intense heat, and the earth and its works will be burned up. Since all these things are to be destroyed in this way, what sort of people ought you to be in holy conduct and godliness, . . . So then, dear friends, since you are looking forward to this, make every effort to be found spotless, blameless and at peace with him. (2 Pet. 3:9-11, NASB, vs. 14, NIV)

> We fall into the need for revival because we slowly let self and sin have its way with us. The little tolerations of the flesh send us into captivity.

Revival means that God renews His patience toward you and you renew "every effort." He wants you to repent; He wants you to get back to 2 Peter 3:11. So many stop revival fires by their unholy "conduct" and lack of "godliness." They simply refuse to deny self enough to get to a place of reconciliation with God.

HARD WORK

We fall into the need for revival because we slowly let self and sin have its way with us. The little tolerations of the flesh send us into captivity.[3] The small justifications and defensiveness concerning our sin send us into a foreign land. All of our talk about conviction of sin, self-righteous talk of demanding righteousness, only causes us to deceive ourselves. That tough sermon our pastor gave was really a dodge that kept us from taking sin seriously.[4]

As a result of this, revival becomes a slow process. If God were to give us revival quickly and easily, we would again take for granted His love for us. We did that before He sent us into captivity and God will not permit it to happen again. God delays revival so that we might take sin seriously and never allow ourselves to be taken captive again. Plus, in order to fix the shattered relationships and messes we have created, it will take much work. This was true when we first came to the Lord and much more so after restoration. Revival, like salvation, is a difficult matter.

> . . . and if it is with difficulty that the righteous is saved, what will become of the godless man and the sinner? (1 Pet. 4:18b NASB)

Listen to the Lord and what He says about revival and never again will you fall prey to those who preach easy wide-road revival. Pray to the Lord to delay His peace in your life that you might not ever "return to folly" again. "Hear what God the Lord" will say about His revival and His peace. Only if we do this, will we once again truly see His "glory dwell in our land."

> I will hear what God the Lord will say; For He will speak peace to His people, to His godly ones; But let them *not turn back to folly*.

Surely His salvation is near to those who fear Him, That glory may dwell in our land. (Ps. 85:8-9 NASB, emphasis added)

God makes us wait long and hard for revival so that we might not ever need it again. Remember, the need for revival results from deep sin. I have never needed revival and pray that I never will.[5] I certainly have needed refreshing in the Lord,[6] but never revival. We need refreshment when we have been emptied out in doing the Lord's work. Revival on the other hand, comes from the need to revive the new life in us once again.[7] Revival calls for slow, painful, agonizing hard work. Revival means the returning again to the pangs of childbirth. Revival allows God to put us back on the cross, to once again drive in the nails and drain us of self. However, like one who has been hurt before as God attempted to crucify self the first time, it is harder at first to endure the pain again. Like a wound that will not heal because we keep hurting the same spot over and over. It is as if a woman failed to give birth the first time only to start all over again to give birth to the same child a second time.

> If revival happens in your life, you can expect moments of rest followed by a new resurgence of conviction of sin.

My dear children, for whom I am again in the pains of childbirth until Christ is formed in you, . . . (Gal. 4:19)

If revival happens in your life, you can expect moments of rest followed by a new resurgence of conviction of sin. During this conviction, God waits to see if you will repent with "godly sorrow"[8] to what He has already shown you. Why should He show you more when you will not respond to the little bit placed before you? Why should you look for more sin, when you haven't repented fully over the old sins? But how people love to delude themselves. They think that if they are always look-ing for the causes of sin in their life, God will accept them. God wants your repentance, not your self-analyzing!

> God sends pain with revival because our flesh must be crucified. In fact, the joy of revival stops from time to time so that God can let you die a bit more to sin.

Again, you will rest for a mo-ment, only to be convicted of some new sin that needs to be dealt with immediately. You must keep in "step with the Spirit"[9] and repent fully, or the new life will not form in you again. If you don't keep in step, the revival will fail in your life. You must place your feet in the footsteps that God will mark out for you.

> Since we live by the Spirit, let us keep in step with the Spirit. (Gal. 5:25)

God sends pain with revival because our flesh must be crucified. In fact, the joy of revival stops from time to time so that God can let you die a bit more to sin. Just think how self-righteous and puffed up you would become if God gave you the fullness of Him back all at once. Most people are too difficult to live with when they think they have a little bit of correctness in the Lord. Think what kind of monster they would be if God really gave them His Spirit.

We see this happening in the fourth chapter of Ezra. Opposition to the revival took place and the building of the temple stopped. God allows opposition to come against us to remind us we must deal with the sin in our lives. Much is at stake and God does not waste a second of any hour in the day. If He has stopped the flow of progress in your revival, stop, search your heart, wait for Him, and repent of what He shows you. If you see no obvious sin, read the Word and build yourself up in the faith,[10] so that you might be ready for the next work. For if this revival does not take root and stick, you have little hope of salvation.

> But you, beloved, building yourselves up on your most holy faith; praying in the Holy Spirit; . . . (Jude 1:20 NASB)

CHAPTER EIGHT

WANTING TO HELP—
THE OPPOSITION

NOTE WELL IN EZRA 4:1-3 THAT OPPOSITION FIRST COMES IN the guise of help. These enemies are the kind who agree with the message of the cross, but live a lie—who accept the notions about the crucified life, but still live for self in the name of Jesus. These individuals have no clue as to their spiritual poverty and become your worst enemy, once the Light is shone on their true condition.

These men claimed to want to only help with this revival, and many others who hate the cross will be glad to help you repent. Be cautious of the religious who try to compel you to come down off the cross in order to save self. There are many and their voices are loud.

> Those who passed by hurled insults at him, shaking their heads and saying, "So! You who are going to destroy the temple and build it in three days, come down from the cross and save your-self!" (Mark 15:29-30)

There will be many false Christians who will want to help with the revival happening in your church, ministry, or life. They come with all the right sounding words. They will talk of sacrifice and love for God's Word but know nothing or little of the crucified life.[1] They are the type that agree with everything that is said about the gospel and even applaud correct doctrine but know nothing of the crucified life. They will say "for we, like you, seek your God."

> There will be many false Christians who will want to help with the revival happening in your church, ministry, or life.

... they approached Zerubbabel and the heads of fathers' households, and said to them, "Let us build with you, for we, like you, seek your God; and we have been sacrificing to Him since the days of Esarhaddon king of Assyria, who brought us up here." (Ezra 4:2 NASB)

Only those who know the cross of Christ in their lives will see through them and reject their offers. Remember, two thieves hung next to Jesus on the cross. Both cried for salvation, but only one asked for true redemption. The wicked thief wanted salvation *from* the cross, while the good thief embraced the crucified life.[2]

Of course, once you reject Satan or the world, these false Christians will turn on you. Remember, one sign of revival is the judging and rejecting of those who worship the Lord in name only.[3] At this point, God tested the Israelite people to see if they had truly fallen in love with Him, or only in love with revival.[4] Those more in love with their cause, church, or ministry will accept just about anyone's offer to help. However, those truly in love with Jesus love His righteousness more than the cause and unrighteous offers of help.

Wait on the Lord to begin revival again. Don't become discouraged when He delays or lets the opposition have its way with you. God wants to make sure that when He pours out His Spirit fully at the end of revival, you are totally ready to let go of self.

> Then work on the house of God in Jerusalem ceased, and it was stopped until the second year of the reign of Darius king of Persia. (Ezra 4:24 NASB)

When revival pauses, search your heart, build yourself up in the Word, and look for unrepented sin in your life. Ask the Lord if you have stopped it or if this is just a pause before going on to the heights. Be assured that if you ask God in faith during these moments of trials, He will give you wisdom.

> Consider it all joy, my brethren, when you encounter various trials, knowing that the testing of your faith produces endurance. And let endurance have its perfect result, that you may be perfect and complete, lacking in nothing. But if any of you lacks wisdom, let him ask of God, who gives to all men generously and without reproach, and it will be given to him. But let him ask in faith without any doubting, for the one who doubts is like the surf of the sea driven and tossed by the wind. (James 1:2-6 NASB)

We must learn to wait on the Lord for all and to let go of self-action that works for God. Revival brings the hard work of waiting upon God.

WAITING ON GOD

We must learn to wait on the Lord for all and to let go of self-action that works for God. Revival brings the hard work of waiting upon God. Like Lazarus, though sick and dying, we must wait for Jesus to come to us. Although He loves us, He must linger, that we might be fully dead to ourselves.

> Now Jesus loved Martha, and her sister, and Lazarus. When therefore He heard that he was sick, He stayed then two days longer in the place where He was. (John 11:5-6 NASB)

Do not rush the work of revival. To do so brings self-will that tries to form God into what we want. Demanding revival only fashions it into an idol. Never force revival with human preaching and prayer, but in humility wait upon the Lord who works all good things in His time. After all, revival returns us to know that God is really God. Revival is not the returning of your peace, comfort, or assurance of salvation; rather it is the returning of God in your life. Satan will give you peace, comfort, and assurance if that is all you are after.

Revival drives you to enter the "Sabbath rest" of God where you learn to wait upon God for everything. Waiting on God is proven by the fact a man increases His obedience to the Word. After all, the acid test of a man's Christianity is his acceptance of scriptures that he doesn't like. It is proven by his obedience to the scriptures he does not find comfortable.

CHAPTER NINE

REVIVAL RESUMED

R EVIVAL, OR THE REBUILDING OF GOD'S TEMPLE, TOOK OVER FIFTEEN years. During those years of work and waiting, the Israelites searched their hearts and saw more sin in their lives. At the end, they finally arrived to a place where they would call sin, "sin." They knew now, not with head knowledge, their unworthiness for God to be with them. God had, however, over the years worked His convincing power in them. But now in God's timing, with God's permission, the people once again had to act on sheer faith to rebuild. The

> Instead, they became a "worm" that could only by God's power do anything.

prophets encouraged the people to begin, for they, in true humility, did not feel worthy. Gone was the self-effort that seeks to lift oneself up in the Lord. Gone was the self-justification of why they should do the work of God. Instead, they became a "worm"[1] that could only by God's power do anything. The new life drew closer, but they still had to labor until God knew they were fully ready for Him.

When the prophets, Haggai the prophet and Zechariah the son of Iddo, prophesied to the Jews who were in Judah and Jerusalem, in the name of the God of Israel, who was over them, then Zerubbabel the son of Shealtiel and Jeshua the son of Jozadak arose and began to rebuild the house of God which is in Jerusalem; and the prophets of God were with them supporting them. At that time Tattenai, the governor of the province beyond the River, and Shethar-bozenai and their colleagues came to them and spoke to them thus, "Who issued you a decree to rebuild this temple and to finish this structure?" Then we told them accordingly what the names of the men were who were reconstructing this building. But the eye of their God was on the elders of the Jews, and they did not stop them until a report should come to Darius, and then a written reply be returned concerning it. (Ezra 5:1-5 NASB)

Did you notice "God's eye" in the passage above? Those eyes of God were upon the "elders" and upon the leadership. Now God looked upon them with favor because the people were willing once again to listen to His teachers. God could now look upon them with favor because they were doing His work from a pure heart. The leaders were willing now to pay the cost of leadership. They were willing to stand up and to do the work and become men of "courage." Although the enemy put them on the spot by asking for their names, they continued the work. Even though men would say, "So you support that church and their message of the cross? What is your name and what part do you have in that church?" they were not ashamed to share in that suffering.[2]

Then we asked those elders and said to them thus, "Who issued you a decree to rebuild this temple and to finish this structure?" We also asked them their names so as to inform you, and that we might write down the names of the men who were at their head. And thus they answered us, saying, "We are the servants of the God of heaven and earth and are rebuilding the temple that was built many years ago, which a great king of Israel built and finished. But because our fathers had provoked the God of heaven to wrath, He gave them into the hand of Nebuchadnezzar king of Babylon, the Chaldean, who destroyed this temple and deported the people to Babylon." (Ezra 5:9-12 NASB)

A sign of revival happens when a person confesses sin in waves over several years and sees himself clearly. A person desiring revival greatly needs to repent and receive a lot of correction, much like a young Christian convicted of sin when first beginning to walk with the Lord. A church, ministry, or person who speaks of revival, but doesn't have this type of lowliness, lies.

> Constantly people today falsely build themselves up by filling themselves up with Christian music, radio, novels, and Bible study, rather than letting God crucify them unto death.

How faithful the people remained in Ezra's time. Every time they had to stop, they confessed their sin and humbled themselves before men and God (Ezra 5:12). Today the vast sea of self-righteous Christians would say, "I already confessed that, so I know I am being blessed. I don't need your rebuke, correction or encouragement." The people of Ezra's time humbled themselves to their enemies. Constantly people today falsely build themselves up by filling themselves up with Christian music, radio, novels, and Bible study,[3] rather than letting God crucify them unto death.

You can often tell this in people by the fact they always seem so surprised they committed the same sin when confronted the next time. They are shocked that you would even come to them. Their cry is not a revival cry, but a whine like, "I thought I was doing better," or "I am really trying." Of course, this is after they have shared every excuse and reason under the Son for their sin.

THE SURGE

Since the Israelites had been faithful in God's true revival up to this point in responding to God's leading in revival, God could surge ahead. Like the final push a women gives in childbirth, the Israelites completed the temple and the new life was ready for delivery. The crown of reward, for their waiting upon God's revival, was ready for placement on their heads. They had persevered[4] over the years in this matter called "revival," and soon the people would gather in the harvest of reconciliation. Without this perseverance, you will never gain the harvest from the fruit called "revival."

> But the seed on good soil stands for those with a noble and good heart, who hear the word, retain it, and *by persevering* produce a crop. (Luke 8:15, emphasis added)

The New Life drew near to giving birth in the Israelites, and this time they treasured it and would not let go. They praised God for His mercy and wisdom. Now that they had labored and sacrificed so much, God could pour out His abundant provision. In Ezra 6:4, we read that the cost of building the temple was paid out of the "royal treasury," and with great speed, they finished everything. All those long delaying years were made up for in months. All those months that seemed futile were overcome in an instant.

How many among us would have fallen away long ago? The sacrifice and slow progress might have been too much and in our hearts, would have stopped loving the Lord long ago. Blessed are those who labor, sacrifice, and love God even when there is no cause to do so.[5] But now the people were ready and God moved very quickly, just like labor and birth. A woman feels that it takes forever to give birth, but the baby comes in a matter of moments at the end of labor. As Ezra 6:9 says, "without delay" "taxes" were gathered and the work completed.

Do you see the irony? The taxes that had been a source of burden and enslavement now paid for their freedom. The discipline had become a source of joy and renewal. Likewise, those who had fallen away from the Lord, or perished in the Lord, had for years paid the necessary taxes for the revival to come. Everything at the end began to come together for the good.[6] For God is able to use captivity by false churches for our good. God is able to work good now, even when in the past we were content to fellowship with those who loved whitewash more than holiness—if we will repent.

The opposition, who had for so long hindered and stopped the work, had to pay for the work's completion (Ezra 6:7-10). The opposition that had for so long tormented the workers and taunted them, now were threatened with punishment (Ezra 6:11). A punishment, like the cross, where the offender would be "impaled" on his house came to anyone who got in the way. The cross which brought life would become death to the troublemaker. Those who gossiped about the Israelites' sin and shame[7] would be threatened with the power of the cross that overcomes the wicked. God defended the Israelites and moved with an even quicker pace to bless them with full reconciliation because they had proven themselves faithful.[8] As Ezra 6:12 says, it was done with "all diligence!"

Then King Darius issued a decree, and search was made in the archives, where the treasures were stored in Babyon. And in Ecbatana in the fortress, which is in the province of Media, a scroll was found and there was written in it as follows: "Memorandum— In the first year of King Cyrus, Cyrus the king issued a decree: 'Concerning the house of God at Jerusalem, let the temple, the place where the sacrifices are offered, be rebuilt and let its foundations be retained, its height being 60 cubits and its width 60 cubits; with three layers of huge stones, and one layer of timbers. And let the cost be paid from the royal treasury.' " (Ezra 6:1-4 NASB)

Those who steal the promises of God and His provisions from you will discover to their dismay, that they have only been guarding them for you. Blessed are those who can wait on God when others steal their promises or discourage them; repent and the treasure will be returned to you.

" 'And also let the gold and silver utensils of the temple of God, which Nebuchadnezzar took from the temple in Jerusalem and brought to Babylon, be returned and brought to their places in the temple in Jerusalem; and you shall put *them* in the house of God.' Now *therefore*, Tattenai, governor of *the province* beyond the River, Shethar-bozenai, and your colleagues, the officials of *the provinces* beyond the River, keep away from there. Leave this work on the house of God alone; let the governor of the Jews and the elders of the Jews rebuild this house of God on its site. Moreover, I issue a decree concerning what you are to do for these elders of Judah in the rebuilding of this house of God: the full cost is to be paid to these people from the royal treasury out of the taxes of *the provinces* beyond the River, and that without delay." (Ezra 6:5-8 NASB)

From those whom the priest had only received opposition in the past, the priest could now demand anything needed for "acceptable sacrifices" to the Lord. As we are promised in the New Testament, if we obey God, asking according to His will, He will hear and answer.[9] During captivity no prayers were answered, but now all they needed to do was ask. Finally the promise of Jesus was theirs.[10]

"And whatever is needed, both young bulls, rams, and lambs for a burnt offering to the God of heaven, and wheat, salt, wine, and anointing oil, as the priests in Jerusalem request, *it* is to be given to them daily without fail, that they may offer acceptable sacrifices to the God of heaven and pray for the life of the king and his sons." (Ezra 6:9-10 NASB)

> Blessed are those who can wait on God when others steal their promises or discourage them.

God once again made known the power of the cross. Let all who get in the way of it be "impaled on it," destroying their religious house and all it stands for. To us who are being saved, the cross is power.[11] For those who get in the way, they will be "crushed."[12]

"And I issued a decree that any man who violates this edict, a timber shall be drawn from his house and he shall be impaled on it and his house shall be made a refuse heap on account of this. And may the God who has caused His name to dwell there overthrow any king or people who attempts to change *it*, so as to destroy this house of God in Jerusalem. I, Darius, have issued *this* decree, let *it* be carried out with all diligence!" Then Tattenai, the governor of *the province* beyond the River, Shethar-bozenai, and their colleagues carried out *the decree* with all diligence, just as King Darius had sent. And the elders of the Jews were successful in building through the prophesying of Haggai the prophet and Zechariah the son of Iddo. And they finished building according to the command of the God of Israel and the decree of Cyrus, Darius, and Artaxerxes king of Persia. And this temple was completed on the third day of the month Adar; it was the sixth year of the reign of King Darius. (Ezra 6:11-15 NASB)

This revival of the temple was completed according to the "command of God." Only when God says revival is complete can people speak of having "had" a revival in their life or church.

The people had finally listened to the prophets and preachers and were willing to walk in joyful obedience to all that God required of them. They submitted to God's discipline and He rewarded in full. The temple was ready and the last blowing wind of revival came with a mighty rush. They would receive the Passover lamb anew in their lives. Let us not dare take the Lord's supper during revival until we too have permission from God.[13] Let us "purify" ourselves and let it be said of us that "all of them were pure" before we partake of the Passover Lamb again. If a church has let the revival fires do their work, then they shall have a whole group of men "pure," unified and ready for service. Blessed is such a church!

> If a church has let the revival fires do their work, then they shall have a whole group of men "pure," unified and ready for service. Blessed is such a church!

And the exiles observed the Passover on the fourteenth of the first month. For the priests and the Levites had purified themselves together; all of them were pure. Then they slaughtered the Passover *lamb* for all the exiles, both for their brothers the priests and for themselves. (Ezra 6:19-20 NASB)

As we would now expect, in Ezra 6:21 we read of even more repentance. Revival caused encouragement and more conviction of sin. This is God's way—rest and then repentance, some more rest and then more repentance—until revival finishes its lasting work.

For thus the Lord God, the Holy One of Israel, has said, "In repentance and rest you shall be saved, In quietness and trust is your strength." But you were not willing, . . . (Isa. 30:15 NASB)

Don't be fooled by revival that inspires for the moment and then stops. If you need revival, it will take some time to finish its way in you. You will feel encouraged and then discouraged. God doesn't want you to return to your sin, so you must take things slowly in this matter called revival. Don't rush to get out from under the weight of God's conviction. Though it may take years of being under conviction, if you continue to hang on the cross, a resurrected life will be given to you. Take in the joy the Lord wants you to have, but know that repentance and sorrow wait right around the corner. Only those who purify themselves in this kind of Godly revival will find themselves reconciled to God. All others will fall by the wayside and go straight to hell when they die.

And the sons of Israel who returned from exile and all those who had separated themselves from the impurity of the nations of the land to *join* them, to seek the Lord God of Israel, ate *the Passover*. And they observed the Feast of Unleavened Bread seven days with joy, for the Lord had caused them to rejoice, and had turned the heart of the king of Assyria toward them to encourage them in the work of the house of God, the God of Israel. (Ezra 6:21-22 NASB)

Do you see how they had "separated themselves" from the "impurity" of the world? Do you see how "seven days of joy" followed their obedience—a joy "caused" by God?[14] Not the joy we see in the church today that comes from self-imposed revival worship. This separation is "pure religion" in God's sight.[15] Joy without obedience is nothing more than golden calf worship in the name of the Lord.[16]

They had now tasted the true "festival" of the Lord that we, as New Testament Christians, are privileged to continue. This festival of joy is the judging and disfellowshipping of others who refuse to honestly repent of sin.[17] It is a love for all that demands holy behavior, from the heart in the Lord. This command brings joy to those who love the Lord. It celebrates the highest and holiest order in God.

Clean out the old leaven, that you may be a new lump, just as you are *in fact* unleavened. For Christ our Passover also has been sacrificed. Let us therefore celebrate the feast, not with old leaven, nor with the leaven of malice and wickedness, but with the unleavened bread of sincerity and truth. I wrote you in my letter not to associate with immoral people; I *did* not at all *mean* with the immoral people of this world, or with the covetous and swindlers, or with idolaters; for then you would have to go out of the world. But actually, I wrote to you not to associate with any so-called brother if he should be an immoral person, or covetous, or an

idolater, or a reviler, or a drunkard, or a swindler—not even to eat
with such a one. For what have I to do with judging outsiders? Do
you not judge those who are within *the church?* But those who are
outside, God judges. REMOVE THE WICKED MAN FROM AMONG YOUR-
SELVES. (1 Cor. 5:7-13 NASB)

Until we want our hearts purified so that our love becomes sin-
cere and based on His truth, we can never expect God to work revival
in our lives. Until we too decide to separate ourselves from worldly
Christians and from unclean things in the world,[18] we will never
find this celebration a joy. Until we judge our brothers who refuse to
repent of sin, we cannot expect God to meet us for fellowship. If you
or your church is in revival, then God's Spirit should have led you
not to eat lunch with certain "Christians." If this has not happened,
don't even dare take the word "revival" on your lips. Little wonder
they could celebrate the Passover with the joy God had given them,
for they obeyed from the heart.

GOD'S FAVOR – THE PEOPLE'S HUMILITY

Revival robs us of our self-confidence. When God showed the
Israelites kindness (Ezra 7:1-28), they no longer took Him for granted.
Revival works a deep seated fear in us not to sin again, and it shows
in one's life. It works a quietness that the emotional revivalist knows
nothing about.

As God continued to move forward to the day of reconciliation, leaders were sought out by God. For over the years, each man
had been at his home quietly repenting, reading the scriptures and
preparing himself for the work of the Lord. Then Ezra, in God's
timing, moved out across the land to find men worthy for leadership (Ezra 8:1-20). What was amazing—and this makes revival

amazing—Ezra found men ready for leadership. How we need true revival today, for it is a rare thing indeed to find leaders who know the way of the cross. We have an abundance of so-called teachers around, but very few qualified in the way of the crucified life.

> How we need true revival today, for it is a rare thing indeed to find leaders who know the way of the cross. We have an abundance of so-called teachers around, but very few qualified in the way of the crucified life.

How humble the Israelite leaders were in the midst of a true, godly revival, unlike today where revival means the sin of arrogance in the name of the Lord. Today's revival makes fun of the devil and gains a few more members for the church. Today's revival is nothing more than fun, frolicking, and revelry. The Israelite worshippers were humbled and allowed themselves to continue to be humbled even more. As a result, they fasted to ensure that God would complete His revival. They needed God's protection on their journey through revival and knew that His anger could flare in a moment.[19] Let us take warning that the closer we get to the end of revival, the greater the danger it might stop. Indeed, Satan had little reason to bother with you until you started to walk in God's revival. Therefore, don't be shocked when, just at the point of birth, Satan rises up to try to halt everything.[20] Satan does not want God glorified or you reconciled.

Stopped by the enemy, by the world or by old stubborn ways, the Israelites had learned that God's love remains with those who seek Him only with "all" their hearts.[21] (God only gives the Holy Spirit to those who obey Him by way of denying self.) So that is exactly what they did—they sought God.

> Then I proclaimed a fast there at the river of Ahava, that we might humble ourselves before our God to seek from Him a safe journey for us, our little ones, and all our possessions. For I was ashamed to request from the king troops and horsemen to protect us from the enemy on the way, because we had said to the king, "The hand of our God is favorably disposed to all those who seek Him, but His power and His anger are against all those who forsake Him." So we fasted and sought our God concerning this *matter,* and He listened to our entreaty. (Ezra 8:21-23 NASB)

Little wonder that God "listened" to their "entreaty." They feared and loved the Lord in a new way they could never have imagined.

Revival renews our fear and trust in the Lord. A revival that does not produce this certainly does not come from God.

> So the church throughout all Judea and Galilee and Samaria enjoyed peace, being built up; and, *going on in the fear of the Lord* and in the comfort of the Holy Spirit, it continued to increase. (Acts 9:31 NASB, emphasis added)

The first church went "on" in the "fear of the Lord." If you desire to be revived again in the Lord, this must happen in your life. Blessed are those who know this, for God will listen to their "entreaty" and bless their journey to the place of reconciliation. God will bless the church that lives in the fear of the Lord. They will never need revival.

Look at Ezra 8:22 and see what they felt ashamed of and what they used to rely upon. Revival causes us to reject the help of man. Those experiencing revival in the Lord no longer look for sympathy from the world. No longer did the Israelites whine to others around them about their captivity and how rough the cross weighed in their lives.[22] Indeed, they felt ashamed at how much in the past they relied upon the self-help books, sermons, the flattering brothers and sisters, and the many preachers who reassured them they were okay in the Lord and to not take sin too seriously.[23] They poured contempt on their declarations of innocence and reliance on others for encouragement. They finally admitted their sin and stopped trying to change their own lives and "ways," in a way they found pleasurable. They stopped listening to those "bold" pastors who make light of sin.

> . . . you say, "I am innocent; he is not angry with me." But I will pass judgment on you because you say, "I have not sinned." Why do you go about so much, changing your ways? You will be disappointed by Egypt as you were by Assyria. (Jer. 2:35-36)

Oh, the arrogance of those in the church today who remain in sinful rest and at peace with God that they cannot detect sin any longer. Why should they, after all, confess sin again and pray for protection with fasting? God had blessed them and started revival in their lives long ago. Those with this attitude forfeit the revival that could have been theirs—all because they have no fear about coming before the Lord or calling upon the salvation of the Lord.

> So then, my beloved, just as you have always obeyed, not as in my presence only, but now much more in my absence, work out your salvation with fear and trembling; (Phil. 2:12 NASB)

THE DAY OF RECONCILIATION WITH GOD

The work of revival in Israel drew near to completion and the fruit of revival was ready for harvesting. The baby was about to be delivered. The people looked forward to getting on with the normal every day walk with God. The New Life drew near to give birth in them. They were ready to get in a place before the Lord where revival would never be needed again. God prepared to tell them they were fully restored and could walk in confidence again with Him. Sweet fellowship with God would once again be theirs.

They had waited long for this day. They submitted and learned to shut up and listen to the Lord and His teachers.[24] They came to know how worthless they stood before God.[25] If you return to the Lord and need to be revived, you will find no quick fix. You have much to undo, by the Lord's direction, in His way and in His timing. As you shall see, the people came to learn that those who have sinned to the point that they need revival know this cannot happen in "a day." They had finally learned this one important lesson—revival does not happen in a day. Yet today how many ignore their sins, telling themselves and others that they have already "confessed it to God." How

> To agree with the scriptures or about a sin in your life means nothing unless repentance matches the agreement.

many think they are doing good in the Lord because they flatter the prophet of God saying, "You are right about my sin," as if agreement constituted holiness. Listen, everyone in hell agrees about their sin. To be sure, those in hell are clear on that matter. To agree with the scriptures or about a sin in your life means nothing unless repentance matches the agreement. Without the cross such sermons are "no more than one who sings love songs with a beautiful voice." They make you feel righteous, but self is still intact.

> As for you, son of man, your countrymen are talking together about you by the walls and at the doors of the houses, saying to each other, "Come and hear the message that has come from the Lord." My people come to you, as they usually do, and sit before you to listen to your words, but they do not put them into practice. With their mouths they express devotion, but their hearts are greedy for unjust gain. Indeed, to them you are nothing more than one who sings love songs with a beautiful voice and plays an instrument well, for they hear your words but do not put them into practice. (Ezek. 33:30-32)

Everything was in place; everyone stood in their proper position and role in the Lord. Hearts were prepared and waiting. Souls were fearful and rejoicing. God's house had all its provisions and the temple was completed. The years had done their work and the people waited for God to act.[26] If you will not respond and obey—for God only gives the Holy Spirit to those who "obey" Him—then don't dare expect revival.

> We are witnesses of these things; and so is the Holy Spirit, whom God has given to those who *obey Him*. (Acts 5:32, emphasis added)

Yet, there was one final blow of conviction and repentance before reconciliation could take place. Just as women must give one final push for the baby to be delivered, don't be surprised if at the end of the journey, you discover one last big thing that needs repentance. Yet, how many quickly say, "I am fine in the Lord!" at the first sign of God's moving. How they use small conviction to justify the hiding of other sin. How quickly they justify their actions when someone corrects them when they first return to the Lord or He works a little peace. When they do this, they lay themselves wide open for captivity again or—even worse—hell.

CHAPTER TEN

THE ACID TEST

N OW, AFTER YEARS OF REPENTING, THE ACID TEST REVEALS WHO really loves the Lord and to whom God can grant the New Life. All their "small" steps of repentance have led up to this day and moment. Think of a mother who gives birth. Think of all the "little" things that must be done. The eating of proper foods every day, the joy, the anxiety, the preparation of the room, the selection of clothing, choosing names, a thousand and one things thought of and done every day. A good mother must order her life, do all she can, run the course marked out for pregnant mothers and trust the Lord.

If the Isarelites had failed at this point, they would have lost everything they had worked for.[1] In order to pass this all important test, you must confess your sin and self fully once again. Think of it, over fifteen years and it still ends with more confession of sin. Are you willing? It appears that some of the priests, like our pastors of today, had delayed their full repentance, and it came as a shock to Ezra. He had thought that by this time, all would have repented; that after all God had done, and the mercy He had shown, certainly they would have taken care of this matter; that after all the sacrifices they had performed, surely no sin like this would be found in their lives. Zeal in work often blinds us to sins. This explains why God will often remove work, especially ministry work, from a man. It explains why God will at times remove worship services from us. During those quiet, slow and boring times, God will allow sin to rise to the surface for you to deal with. If you are sick and unable to work, or hemmed in for some other reason by the hand of God, then resolve to "watch your life and doctrine closely."[2] Rid yourself of distractions and ignore fleshly discomforts—make every effort to seek the Lord.

> How sad that the church leaders of today remain loaded down with the sins of loving sports, pleasure, other women (divorce and remarriage), money, and self in general.

Everything comes to a halt because, as the verse below says, "The people of Israel and the priests and the Levites have not separated themselves from the peoples of the lands." Let us halt also before revival goes any further and ask ourselves, "How separate am I from the world? How separate am I in holidays, dress, money . . . in all ways from the custom of those around me?"

This especially applies to leaders because they set the example, and as verse 2 below states, "the hands of the princes and the rulers have been foremost in this unfaithfulness." How sad that the church leaders of today remain loaded down with the sins of loving sports, pleasure, other women (divorce and remarriage), money, and self in general. If ever a passage applied today, this is it:

Now when these things had been completed, the princes approached me, saying, "The people of Israel and the priests and the Levites have not separated themselves from the peoples of the lands, according to their abominations, those of the Canaanites, the Hittites, the Perizzites, the Jebusites, the Ammonites, the Moabites, the Egyptians, and the Amorites. For they have taken some of their daughters as wives for themselves and for their sons, so that the holy race has intermingled with the peoples of the lands; indeed, the hands of the princes and the rulers have been foremost in this unfaithfulness." And when I heard about this matter, I tore my garment and my robe, and pulled some of the hair from my head and my beard, and sat down appalled. Then everyone who trembled at the words of the God of Israel on account of the unfaithfulness of the exiles gathered to me, and I sat appalled until the evening offering. (Ezra 9:1-4 NASB)

When you see such sin, do you "pull some" of your "hair" out? Have you "sat" down to think about these sins until you feel "appalled" by the inspiration of the Holy Spirit? Only those who become "appalled" will have wisdom from God as to how such sin should be dealt with. Only the one who weeps will know from God what is holy to do.[3] To put this in New Testament terms, has God been able by the Holy Spirit to work the following passage in your life?

For, as I have often told you before and now say again even with tears, many live as enemies of the cross of Christ. (Phil. 3:18)

Are you flowing with tears because so many claim to be Christians but are really "enemies of the cross of Christ"? Do you count them as your enemies? Do you warn others? Only those who "tremble" at God's Word and who do not "deny him by their actions"[4] will experience revival and rally to God's true teachers. Everyone else will find teachers who suit their needs. Only after Ezra sat down to think about these sins did he get on his knees to pray about them. How many pray so haphazardly about sin because they do not want to sit down and look at sin in a serious manner. How easily we pray for others about their sins without first

> When was the last time you felt "embarrassed" before the Lord because of other's sins?

sitting down before the Lord to become appalled as He is appalled. How few of us can claim to be "embarrassed" as Ezra at the sin in other's lives. When was the last time you felt "embarrassed" before the Lord because of other's sins? You are probably not even embarrassed by your own sins, let alone concerned about someone else's sins.[5] All you care about is yourself and your personal salvation. This is why so many who talk about sins in the church, do so little about it by the power of the Spirit. Only when we feel "embarrassed" like this will we be fit to "stretch out" our hands and pray from our "knees" about the sins of others.

> But at the evening offering I arose from my humiliation, even with my garment and my robe torn, and I fell on my knees and stretched out my hands to the Lord my God; and I said, "O my God, I am ashamed and embarrassed to lift up my face to Thee, my God, for our iniquities have risen above our heads, and our guilt has grown even to the heavens. Since the days of our fathers to this day we have been in great guilt, and on account of our iniquities we, our kings and our priests have been given into the hand of the kings of the lands, to the sword, to captivity, and to plunder and to open shame, as it is this day. But now for a brief

moment grace has been shown from the Lord our God, to leave us an escaped remnant and to give us a peg in His holy place, that our God may enlighten our eyes and grant us a little reviving in our bondage." (Ezra 9:5-8 NASB)

In verse 8, we now see for the first time Ezra talking about "grace." For the first time we see the word "revival" ("reviving") used. Naturally, now they can honestly talk about being "enlightened" in the Lord, of really understanding what grace and revival are about. Oh, that God's people would also go to the end of revival, that they too would see that grace provides the power to change, to overcome and to be victorious. Read Titus 2:11-15 below and notice how it instructs us that God's grace gives the power to change. The grace of God, if alive in you, teaches you to say "No" to sin and to "live self-controlled," "upright" and "godly" right now in this "present age." The grace of God gives overcoming power to say "No" to self, and if you don't have this grace, you need revival. Titus states that this is the "grace" that has "appeared to all men." This is what God means by "grace" and it is quite a contrast to what is preached today. How many claim to agree with this grace, but know it not from a position of revival.

> The grace of God, if alive in you, teaches you to say "No" to sin and to "live self-controlled," "upright" and "godly" right now in this "present age."

For the grace of God that brings salvation has appeared to all men. It teaches us to say "No" to ungodliness and worldly passions, and to live self-controlled, upright and godly lives in this present age, while we wait for the blessed hope—the glorious appearing of our great God and Savior, Jesus Christ, who gave himself for us to redeem us from all wickedness and to purify for himself a people that are his very own, eager to do what is good. These, then, are the things you should teach. Encourage and rebuke with all authority. Do not let anyone despise you. (Titus 2:11-15)

This is the grace presented with "all authority," both with encouragement and rebukes, which is exactly what Ezra did.

THE WHOLE CAMP

AS WE SAID AT THE START, REVIVAL IS FOR THE REMNANT OF THE REMnant. The remnant is tested and only an "escaped remnant" stands before the Lord. Be afraid, because few, very few indeed, survive a revival. Revival is the removal of dross, not the gaining of new members. The Israelites stand in the midst of "reviving," yet Ezra trembles that it could all be lost if the people do not repent. Ezra was not selfish or self-centered about revival—he had the love of God in him. He knew that if the whole camp did not repent, then each individual's revival was at stake. Today everyone would walk away too satisfied with themselves to worry about a few folks who will not repent. How little love is in the church today. No one wants to confront sin, but each person is selfishly satisfied if they feel secure in the Lord.

> For we are slaves; yet in our bondage, our God has not forsaken us, but has extended lovingkindness to us in the sight of the kings of Persia, to give us reviving to raise up the house of our God, to restore its ruins, and to give us a wall in Judah and Jerusalem. And

now, our God, what shall we say after this? For we have forsaken Thy commandments, which Thou hast commanded by Thy servants the prophets, saying, "The land which you are entering to possess is an unclean land with the uncleanness of the peoples of the lands, with their abominations which have filled it from end to end and with their impurity. So now do not give your daughters to their sons nor take their daughters to your sons, and never seek their peace or their prosperity, that you may be strong and eat the good things of the land and leave it as an inheritance to your sons forever." And after all that has come upon us for our evil deeds and our great guilt, since Thou our God hast requited us less than our iniquities deserve, and hast given us an escaped remnant as this, shall we again break Thy commandments and intermarry with the peoples who commit these abominations? Wouldst Thou not be angry with us to the point of destruction, until there is no remnant nor any who escape? O Lord God of Israel, Thou art righteous, for we have been left an escaped remnant, as it is this day; behold, we are before Thee in our guilt, for no one can stand before Thee because of this. (Ezra 9:9-15 NASB)

Do you see this? After years of building, sacrificing, repenting, worshipping, and waiting upon God, they conclude, "Behold, we are before Thee in our guilt, for no one can stand before Thee because of this."

Didn't God answer their fasting and prayer? Did not God give them victory to this point? Maybe they were just being too hard on themselves. Would we not, in our foolishness, or in our jealousy of their revival, comfort them and tell them to claim the blood of Jesus?

Would we not point out their sin in our self-righteousness? Instead of repenting, wouldn't we seek to knock the other person down to size? How many are so perverted while in captivity. They want everyone to do poorly in the Lord if they cannot be blessed. Like Cain, they are "downcast" because of their brother's righteousness, until, of course, they can cause them to stumble. If a fellow wanderer in the desert is being blessed in the Lord, it galls them to no end and they must do something about it. And until they make them stumble, they are not happy in the Lord.

However, would not Ezra and his fellow worshippers quote to us the following passages?

> Therefore come out from them and be separate, says the Lord. Touch no unclean thing, and I will receive you. I will be a Father to you, and you will be my sons and daughters, says the Lord Almighty. (2 Cor. 6:17-18)

> Since we have these promises, dear friends, let us purify ourselves from everything that contaminates body and spirit, perfecting holiness out of reverence for God. (2 Cor. 7:1)

So few in the church today can speak of "perfecting holiness" by cleaning up their "spirit" and "body." Today the church, however, constantly says, "All God cares about is the heart." How blessed the Israelites were that they did not have this attitude and realized that the heart is reflected in how a man dresses and behaves.[1] For you see, all the little brokenness and little sins God had shown over the years had prepared them for this day. Similarly, Jesus rebuked

> Pray that you will never need revival and prepare yourself if you do need revival for what God must work to reconcile you.

Peter for three years to prepare him for his denial at the end of those years. For over three years Jesus' rebukes to Peter were mild preparations for getting to the cross. At that point Peter finally despaired of self. In other words, because the people repented of the small things over the years which God showed them, He could deal with all of self. In the same way since Abraham learned to surrender and trust God daily, he could one day be faithful enough to sacrifice his own son. Samson, who learned literally to die to sin, slew more when he died to self than when he was alive.

> Samson said, "Let me die with the Philistines!" Then he pushed with all his might, and down came the temple on the rulers and all the people in it. Thus he killed many more when he died than while he lived. (Judges 16:30)

You too must learn this literally—that you will kill more for the Lord when you die to self than when you are alive. Until that time, like Samson, your passions, fleshly desires, stubbornness, lies, and half-truths will continue to cause you to be taken captive. Consider the quiet time in jail and discipline that Samson had to endure before this revival could take place. Pray that you will never need revival[2] and prepare yourself if you do need revival for what God must work to reconcile you. Samson had to have his eyes gouged out and be bound in chains to learn his lessons. What will it take for you to no longer half-way weep over your sin?

> Those willing to daily repent of the small things will be ready to sacrifice self on the day God calls for the end of revival.

Pray that you will be as the words of Jesus describe: "He who is faithful with little, will be faithful with much."[3] Those willing to daily repent of the small things will be ready to sacrifice self on the day God calls for the end of revival. After all, he who repents of small things, will never again need revival. Blessed is the church who has leaders that can lead the people in this. But as long as you consider short times of weeping as being crucified, even the most Godly leaders will profit you nothing.

DAY OF BIRTH

Does the following sound like the crowning achievement called "revival"? Yet, it is God's revival.

> Now while Ezra was praying and making confession, weeping and prostrating himself before the house of God, a very large assembly, men, women, and children, gathered to him from Israel; for the people wept bitterly. (Ezra 10:1 NASB)

Again, hadn't they wept many times before? Of course they had, but their hearts needed to fill up with the cross of Christ.[4] Sadly, the church often accepts individuals after small tokens of conviction. Counting the cost just does not happen in the church often in the church today[5]—the cost that says we must give up all. Certainly calling the crowd of visitors who come to your church "vipers" is totally unheard of today.[6]

The people of Israel came to this place where they either had to decide to give up all or lose all. Either the baby would be born alive or stillborn. Either they would give that one final push for delivery or kill the baby in the womb. Either the Israelites would have the strength to finish the revival or the revival would become an everlasting disgrace. How many churches and individuals reach the end of revival only to find out they haven't the strength to finish it? They return to their old comfortable religious ways. They get right to the end, having thought all along that this revival is "great," but only gave 99.9% to the Lord. Because of this, they didn't have the strength to deliver the New Life.

> They told him, "This is what Hezekiah says: This day is a day of distress and rebuke and disgrace, as when children come to the point of birth and there is no strength to deliver them." (Isa. 37:3)

They had to send away their own children and wives in order to have the Lord! They had come to a day of decision. Each person had to ask themselves, "Is fellowship with God more valuable than fellowship with my wife, children[7] or with the world?"[8] Put in New Testament terms, they would have to live as "though they are not married,"[9] not look for a wife,[10] and cleanse themselves from the world. What they needed to do was clear, for they had been unified in God's Word and Spirit. No longer were any debates necessary as to what they should repent of. So much time is wasted in the church today because men can't even decide what is sin, let alone how to repent.

> And Shecaniah the son of Jehiel, one of the sons of Elam, answered and said to Ezra, "We have been unfaithful to our God, and have married foreign women from the peoples of the land; yet now there is hope for Israel in spite of this. So now let us make a covenant with our God to put away all the wives and their children, according to the counsel of my lord and of those who tremble at the commandment of our God; and let it be done according to the law." (Ezra 10:2-3 NASB)

If revival comes from God, then let it be "done according to the law," or according to the Word of the Lord. Let your church demonstrate so much obedience that others will call it legalistic. If there is any "hope" left in spite of your church's sins, let each seek the "counsel" of the "godly" and of those who "tremble" at the Word. If you are just one individual in the midst of revival, then seek out those who know what it is to be crucified with Christ and ask for counsel. Beg for it, go out of your way for it, and if they call you a "dog,"[11] all the better. Don't find someone you consider to be your equal in the Lord or someone you can feel comfortable getting advise from. Seek out those more mature in the Lord and demand "counsel." Keep away from anyone who puts obstacles in your way either by their life, doctrine, or words.[12]

> If you are just one individual in the midst of revival, then seek out those who know what it is to be crucified with Christ and ask for counsel. Beg for it, go out of your way for it, and if they call you a "dog," all the better.

OUT IN THE OPEN

No one can mistake it. Boldness and openness mark this type of obedience. If you have to tell someone you are repenting or are being revived, then you are not really repenting! Don't ever say you are "repenting" because everyone will see that in you if it is true. Like Zaccheus, let us not repent quietly, hidden away somewhere. Let us "Arise" and proclaim our repentance by correcting our wrongs four times over. Do you want reconciliation, revival, and salvation from the Lord? Then this is the only way.

And Zaccheus stopped and said to the Lord, "Behold, Lord, half of my possessions I will give to the poor, and if I have defrauded anyone of anything, I will give back four times as much." And Jesus said to him, "Today salvation has come to this house, because he, too, is a son of Abraham." (Luke 19:8-9 NASB)

Let us "stop" everything and claim the day of revival, repenting fully of what God shows us. Let everyone see you "stop" everything, especially ministry work, and tell the Lord how you plan to specifically repent. Make a list of your sins, with scriptures on how to repent and then set out to obey—the Holy Spirit will meet you there. Let all see your shame, your sin, and your repentance. This is where "salvation" is found.

For this is God's way of revival. God blesses those who show "courage"[13] in their repentance. The Israelites repented with so much zeal that they sealed it with an "oath." Since they had resolved to repent, it would be done, and nothing would stop them. In fact, Ezra did not enjoy any fellowship—the "bread" and the "water"—with the Lord until repentance took place. Let no good thing of the Lord that you desire to enjoy keep you from repenting first.[14] Let no good thing keep you from making sure others repent. Do not be selfish and content in the Lord if others do not repent.

"Arise! For this matter is your responsibility, but we will be with you; be courageous and act." Then Ezra rose and made the leading priests, the Levites, and all Israel, take oath that they would do according to this proposal; so they took the oath. Then Ezra rose from before the house of God and went into the chamber of Jehohanan the son of Eliashib. Although he went there, he did not eat bread, nor drink water, for he was mourning over the un-faithfulness of the exiles. (Ezra 10:4-6 NASB)

Encourage your leaders to "Arise!" and deal with sin in each home and family. Invite your pastor into your house and plead with him to point out anything sinful. You read that right, encourage him to "Arise," "act" and be "coura-geous." How many love pastors who mind their own business! You see, before this time, at the start of God's warnings of captivity, they had re-fused those whom He sent. In the scripture above, they pleaded with Ezra to go and confront people with God, but in Isaiah's day they said . . .

> Encourage your leaders to "Arise!" and deal with sin in each home and family.

They say to the seers, "See no more visions!" and to the prophets, "Give us no more visions of what is right! Tell us pleasant things, prophesy illusions. Leave this way, get off this path, and stop con-fronting us with the Holy One of Israel!" (Isa. 30:10-11)

And "Arise" Ezra and the leaders did—so much so that they arose with an "oath." A revival that does not come this way is not of God and will not end in reconciliation with Him. As the passage below declares, anyone who doesn't accept this revival will "forfeit" all he owns in the Lord and be "excluded" from the church.

And they made a proclamation throughout Judah and Jerusalem to all the exiles, that they should assemble at Jerusalem, and that

whoever would not come within three days, according to the counsel of the leaders and the elders, all his possessions should be forfeited and he himself excluded from the assembly of the exiles.
(Ezra 10:7-8 NASB)

Of course, the passage below would say "three days." Jesus was
raised on the third day, and all of scripture points to Him, who He is,
and how He deals with us.

So all the men of Judah and Benjamin assembled at Jerusalem
within the three days. It was the ninth month on the twentieth of
the month, and all the people sat in the open square before the
house of God, trembling because of this matter and the heavy
rain. (Ezra 10:9 NASB)

Of course, revival was "out in the open," in the Light where
everyone could see sin being dealt with. These folks were "walking
in the Light" long before the command was written with ink.[15] Of
course, they were all at church not doing as they pleased on Sunday.
No attendance problem here.[16] Of course, only "men" led in this
revival, since women did not lead in the church.[17] Of course, the
rain sent from God that washed away their sins symbolizes their water
baptism that a long time ago "saved them."[18] God could wash away
their sins because they willingly "trembled" over what they had done
and read each line of scripture with a holy fear. They were now ready
to obey scripture all the way. Indeed, they wanted, with joy, to give
all in order to obey God and to hear His voice once again. Fellowship with God now meant more than anything. The one thing God
had been waiting for, the one thing that would bring full reconciliation and the normal Christian life, they were now willing to do.

These were not foolish virgins who only had enough oil to get them by for a few short hours.[19] Virgins, though they kept themselves pure, were not overflowing with the Holy Spirit and the Word of God. Virgins who were more virtuous than those churches around them[20] but still sadly wanting in the Lord. They were even so noble as to realize they needed to go and buy some more oil. They even set out with great speed and action to buy some oil— they looked like they were repenting. They knew they needed revival, but they had waited too long to allow revival to do its work. Their hearts would never be right. For the only reason they desired more oil sprang from a selfish motive—they only wanted Jesus as their personal Lord and Savior.

They wanted more of the Lord and His righteousness, but it was too late. They thought they had enough oil to get them by and didn't need a thing. They even made it through most of the dark night, and though they felt in their hearts something wasn't right, they considered conviction by the Spirit to be enough. They even ran off and bought more oil because of their need to be closer to Jesus. Let us learn the lesson that being convicted of sin and having some oil is never enough to save one's soul. They had overestimated their standing in the Lord – the first sign of the need for revival.

> But while they were on their way to buy the oil, the bridegroom arrived. The virgins who were ready went in with him to the wedding banquet. And the door was shut. Later the others also came. "Sir! Sir!" they said. "Open the door for us!" But he replied, "I tell you the truth, I don't know you." Therefore keep watch, because you do not know the day or the hour. (Matt. 25:10-13)

CHAPTER TWELVE

WORDS OF COMFORT

O F COURSE, THE ISRAELITES DID NOT HEAR WORDS OF COMFORT, unless you count comfort as being allowed to obey God. They did not hear words of encouragement and peace, unless you count humility the best self-esteem in the world. This was no false prophet preaching in the church who told them how God loved them so they were free to please themselves. This was an honest to goodness godly revival where Ezra went straight for the sin. He demanded that they repent, "make confession," "do His [God's] will" and obey the scriptures. This is not the kind of preacher we want in

> He demanded that they repent, "make confession," "do His [God's] will" and obey the scriptures. This is not the kind of preacher we want in our churches today.

our churches today. This is a godly preacher that demands obedience to the Lord in all things, not just a few select commands.

Then Ezra the priest stood up and said to them, "You have been unfaithful and have married foreign wives adding to the guilt of Israel. Now, therefore, make confession to the Lord God of your fathers, and do His will; and separate yourselves from the peoples of the land and from the foreign wives." Then all the assembly answered and said with a loud voice, "That's right! As you have said, so it is our duty to do." (Ezra 10:10-12 NASB)

What unity among the people that they could all proclaim it was their "duty." They all agreed what to repent of and how to repent. The daily foundation of sacrifice was paying off. They had done their daily "duty,"[1] and now they would be able to do all that God required with a joyful heart. What denial of self we see, what grand righteousness. What overflowing holiness like a "never failing stream"[2] belonged to them. Their acts of righteousness would not stop and start. Where in the past they might do some righteous acts one day, but the next day be full of self. Where once their worship services had been sin, now they would be acts of

> No longer would their weekly Bible studies just be self-help groups that come together and chat about their personal problems . . .

righteousness. At one time you might get a trickle of purity from them if you were lucky, now they would have overflowing righteousness like a "stream." In order to get this righteousness, God had to stop their "assemblies" and send them into captivity. They had submitted to this discipline, and mercy would be theirs in abundance.

I hate, I despise your religious feasts; I cannot stand your assemblies. Even though you bring me burnt offerings and grain offerings, I will not accept them. Though you bring choice fellowship offerings, I will have no regard for them. Away with the noise of your songs! I will not listen to the music of your harps. But let justice roll on like a river, righteousness like a never-failing stream! (Amos 5:21-24)

Now they would be fit to deal with the enemies around them. No longer would they wallow in self-absorption dealing with their petty personal problems and discomforts. No longer would their weekly Bible studies just be self-help groups that come together and chat about their personal problems—the kind of Bible studies that do just enough good deeds and say just enough righteous words to make one feel righteously comfortable in the Lord. Or a Sunday School class where everyone goes around and shares their stupid opinions about what they think God's Word means.[3] They had been willing to tremble with fear, so God allowed them to touch the hem of His garments.[4] They were granted the mind of Christ.

The depth of unity concerning God's Word displays the fruit of revival. God does not grant revival and then leave each man to interpret His Word as he sees fit. That kind of disagreement shows the need for revival, not the result of revival.[5] See how united they were concerning God's Word. Note how they would now listen and submit to the "leaders"[6] God had given them. In fact, in their zeal, they ask that the "leaders represent the whole assembly in this matter." What a change; before captivity they had despised and rejected the authority of God's teachers. Now they embraced and loved those teachers that dealt with sin. In the past, they were powerless to do that which was right, to understand the correct course; now they could run in the way of righteousness. No longer would their deeds not be "complete."

> But there are many people, it is the rainy season, and we are not able to stand in the open. Nor can the task be done in one or two days, for we have transgressed greatly in this matter. "Let our leaders represent the whole assembly and let all those in our cities who have married foreign wives come at appointed times, together with the elders and judges of each city, until the fierce anger of our God on account of this matter is turned away from us." (Ezra 10:13-14 NASB)

How could they talk of God's "fierce anger" and take several days to repent, when He had brought them so far in the rebuilding of the temple? The answer lies in the meaning of true revival. The closer we draw to God, the more we realize the shameful sins in our lives. Those far from God, in need of revival, have little sense of what they do wrong.[7] Those whom God chooses to bring to Himself must come to see sin and self clearly. When the disciples first fell on their knees at the calling of Jesus, they no doubt thought they saw their sins clearly.[8] Little did they know that Jesus would convince them of the futility of self and sin in ways they could not, nor wanted, to imagine.

> The person closest to the cross not only sees his sin and weakness of self clearly, but remains only days away from the resurrected life.

Very often those who talk of God's "fierce anger," and see that anger clearly on His face, stand on the verge of forgiveness. Those who have backslidden and yet talk of taking days, or even years, to repent of a sin draw near to full reconciliation with God. Those who admit they don't really understand one scripture by the enlightened power of the Holy Spirit, will gain the mind of Christ.[9] The person closest to the cross not only sees his sin and weakness of self clearly, but remains only days away from the resurrected life.

Chapter Thirteen

The One Thing

SADLY, MANY PASS THROUGH ALL THE VALLEYS AND TRAVEL ALONG the wind ing roads that lead to the day of revival, only to turn back. They too have prayed, fasted, wept, rejoiced, waited, worked, sacrificed, accepted discipline, and trusted God, but now they can- not do the one thing that would seal revival in their lives. The cost seems too high and now they turn their backs on God—forever. What a waste to come to the end of revival and still remain dead in sin. Dead in sin and self because they "opposed" the last and one thing God demanded of them. Think of it, they gave 99% to God but refused to give 100%. They failed at the greatest command God gave.

> ". . . let our officials act for the whole assembly. Then let every-
> one in our towns who has married a foreign woman come at a set
> time, along with the elders and judges of each town, until the
> fierce anger of our God in this matter is turned away from us."
> Only Jonathan son of Asahel and Jahzeiah son of Tikvah,

supported by Meshullam and Shabbethai the Levite, opposed this. (Ezra 10:14-15)

What made Jesus a Christian while he walked with us? What was the one thing that made Jesus different from the rest of us? And what is the one thing, that if we had it in fullness would make us perfectly like Him?

That one thing is the cross. He carried His cross daily and was crucified to self perfectly every hour and second of every day. Suppose Jesus had done everything God wanted Him to do, except die on the cross. Where would we be? If Jesus had denied Himself in every way that God called Him to all those years, but refused to die on the cross, there would have been no salvation for us. In the same way, if we refuse to be crucified to self by the power of the Holy Spirit how can we be saved? To be sure, this is a salvation apart from works, for it is His working in us. But if we refuse the cross, what hope is there? We must have the same attitude as Christ in order to put our flesh to death.

> Therefore, since Christ has suffered in the flesh, arm yourselves also with the same purpose, because he who has suffered in the flesh has ceased from sin. (1 Pet. 4:1 NASB)

Only those willing to "hate" their very lives will permit God to deal with them so powerfully.

> He who loves his life loses it, and he who hates his life in this world will keep it to life eternal. (John 12:25 NASB)

An individual who does not have this God inspired hatred living in them will refuse the justifying work of the Holy Spirit. For it is this godly hatred that makes one ready to be a disciple of Jesus. This is the word that Jesus speaks to the "large crowds," the religious crowds that were following Him. It is this word "hate" that Jesus "turned" and declared to them.

> Large crowds were traveling with Jesus, and turning to them he said: "If anyone comes to me and does not hate his father and mother, his wife and his children, his brothers and sisters—yes, even his own life—he cannot be my disciple. And anyone who does not carry his cross and follow me cannot be my disciple."(Luke 14:25-27)

> An individual who does not have this God inspired hatred living in them will refuse the justifying work of the Holy Spirit. For it is this godly hatred that makes one ready to be a disciple of Jesus.

If this godly hatred is present, then one is ready to "carry his own cross" and follow Jesus. For those who do not hate their own lives and permit the living God to crucify their sin and self, though they travel many miles with Jesus they refuse to go to the cross of Christ, they will certainly die in Hell.

Now is the time to "wake up," to revive what is about to die. Now is the time to get your soiled garments cleaned so that your name might remain in the book of life. Do you have ears that can hear the call to a whisper revival that God is speaking to the churches today?

> Remember what you have received and heard; and keep it, and repent. If therefore you do not wake up, I will come like a thief, and you will not know at what hour I will come to you. But you

have a few people in Sardis who have not soiled their garments; and they will walk with Me in white, for they are worthy. He who overcomes shall thus be clothed in white garments; and I will not erase his name from the book of life, and I will confess his name before My Father and before His angels. He who has an ear, let him hear what the Spirit says to the churches. (Rev. 3:3-6 NASB)

CHAPTER FOURTEEN

DISCIPLESHIP–TO BEGIN

W HERE DO I BEGIN?" PEOPLE OFTEN ASK ME. THE ANSWER LIES IN the nature of revival. Revival means starting completely over and beginning again—it is new life. A man or woman who is not willing to lay it all at the cross and start from the very beginning is not ready for God's revival. For God's good seed of revival to be planted in you, everything must be plowed up. The ground of your heart must be laid bare and made ready to receive God's seed of revival. To be sure, the old ground that was never plowed must be broken up. For there are many that never received any blessing of His seed. The hard soil, the ground with weeds and the mixed field of wheat and weeds must all be laid bare to the wind, sun, and water that will cause God's seed of revival to produce a harvest of righteousness. That very beginning, the good seed can be examined in my book entitled, *Hating For Jesus*.

> For thus says the Lord to the men of Judah and to Jerusalem, "Break up your fallow ground, and do not sow among thorns." (Jer. 4:3 NASB)

If you are ready for revival, or are prepared to examine yourself to see if you need revival, then *Hating For Jesus* is the next book you may want to read. It is a book for those willing to start with a clean slate. Even if you are strong in the Lord, it will help you to allow the Lord to prune you back so that you will be more fruitful. For you can't just sew on this new "patch" of material and expect it to survive attached to old spiritual ways.

> No one sews a patch of unshrunk cloth on an old garment; otherwise the patch pulls away from it, the new from the old, and a worse tear results. (Mark 2:21 NASB)

Hating for Jesus deals specifically with the very first step everyone must take before they can call themselves a Christian. Indeed, if someone is not living and fully preaching John 12:25 and Luke 14:25–35, then they have no eternal life in them. Take warning, *Hating For Jesus* is not a book for those who do not like the tone of Jesus' offensive cross.

Revival can only be of the living true God if this Holy Spirit inspired hatred is present and growing. *Hating For Jesus* speaks directly to this first issue which must be the issue of issues every day for every Christian.

Everything Said

With all of this said, may you humbly accept the revival that is "according to" His "word." May you be revived, but only according to His living Word.

My soul cleaves to the dust; Revive me according to Thy word. (Ps. 119:25 NASB)

ENDNOTES

INTRODUCTION
1. Ecc. 7:10

CHAPTER ONE – THE WHISPER REVIVAL
1. 2 Cor. 11:33
2. 2 Thess. 2:11
3. Dan. 12:7

CHAPTER TWO – THE CROSS
1. John 12:25, Luke 14:25–35
2. Luke 24:45
3. Ps. 17:14, I John 2:15
4. Order the book, *Hating For Jesus*, WinePress Publishing ISBN# 1-57921-152-6

CHAPTER THREE – RECEIVING THIS REVIVAL
1. James 2:5
2. Ecc. 5:1
3. Rom. 8:17
4. Rom. 12:3

5. Hos. 12:6
6. 2 Cor. 11:23

Chapter Four – A Shameful Thing
1. Heb. 6:11
2. Rom. 12:11
3. 1 Pet. 2:1–2
4. Jer. 19:9
5. Heb. 6:6

Chapter Five – Revival Begins
1. Mark 5:17-20
2. Mark 5:40, This is not to say that the Spirit might lead someone to do a more public miracle, such as when Jesus raised Lazarus from the dead. Rather, it is to call attention to how often Jesus toned the people down rather than causing them to become excited.
3. 1 Cor. 2:4-5 "My message and my preaching were not with wise and persuasive words, but with a demonstration of the Spirit's power, so that your faith might not rest on men's wisdom, but on God's power."
4. John 6:26
5. Luke 14:27 & 14:33
6. Rom. 12:1-2
7. Matt. 4:6
8. Rom. 9:16
9. Acts 5:3, Their first sin was not lying, but keeping back something for self. When we seek to keep things back for ourselves we resort to lying to cover up our lack of surrender.
10. Luke 14:26
11. Matt. 13:44
12. Gal. 5:25
13. 1 John 3:18
14. John 12:10 "So the chief priests made plans to kill Lazarus as well . . . "
15. Mark 4:25
16. Isa. 57:10
17. James 5:16

18. Luke 14:32
19. John 5:16
20. Heb. 12:16-17
21. Jer. 4:3
22. Ezek. 34:18-21
23. Mark 6:51-52
24. 1 Cor. 10:4
25. Ecc. 10:4 "If a ruler's anger rises against you, do not leave your post; calmness can lay great errors to rest."
26. Eph. 4:8-15 "This is why it says: "When he ascended on high, he led captives in his train and gave *gifts* to men." (What does "he ascended" mean except that he also descended to the lower, earthly regions? He who descended is the very one who ascended higher than all the heavens, in order to fill the whole universe.) It was he who gave some to be apostles, some to be prophets, some to be evangelists, and some to be pastors and teachers, to prepare God's people for works of service, so that the body of Christ may be built up until we all reach unity in the faith and in the knowledge of the Son of God and become mature, attaining to the whole measure of the fullness of Christ. Then we will no longer be infants, tossed back and forth by the waves, and blown here and there by every wind of teaching and by the cunning and craftiness of men in their deceitful scheming. Instead, speaking the truth in love, we will in all things grow up into him who is the Head, that is, Christ." (emphasis added)
27. Rom. 12:1-3
28. 1 Thess. 5:21
28. Very often those returning have minds that race with every kind of thought. They must confess this as sin and let God crucify all the anxiety, talk and thoughts they have. They must let the Holy Spirit control their minds if they are to regain the thoughts and peace of the Lord. Beware that usually the pride of wanting to be right on something, after spending so much time in captivity stops the Spirit. Not to mention that years of an undisciplined mind will take its toll on us. "The mind of sinful man is death, but the mind controlled by the Spirit is life and peace" (Rom. 8:6).
30. The more a man allows himself to be rebuked, the more a man responds to those rebukes, the more wisdom he will have from God. See Proverbs 1:23.
31. Mark 6:11

32. Phil. 3:1
33. 1 Sam. 15:23
34. Matt. 5:6
35. Job 42:5-6, Isa. 6:1-7
36. Hos. 12:6
37. 1 Sam. 13
38. Matt. 23:15
39. Ps. 139:17
40. John 17:22
41. Loving people as Jesus did, not with socializing. A love that comes out in gentleness and sometimes in calling our bother and sisters "Satan." See John 13:34, Mark 8:33.
42. How sad that many fill their day with so much Christian music that God cannot find a moment's silence to speak to them. Their "quiet times" are only for 15 minutes in the morning instead of all day.
43. 1 Cor. 11:31
44. Luke 22:42-43 " 'Father, if you are willing, take this cup from me; yet not my will, but yours be done.' An angel from heaven appeared to him and strengthened him." When Jesus reached a point where the cross was beyond human endurance, an angel "strengthened him". It will be the same for those who lay a foundation of sacrifice and move on into the garden. You will be pushed beyond your endurance and be given strength from heaven. In this way, God will be glorified.
45. 1 Cor. 9:27
46. Acts 8:21-22
47. Ps 73:9 "Their mouths lay claim to heaven, and their tongues take possession of the earth."
48. Rom. 9:15-16, Heb. 6:6
49. Ps. 127
50. Num. 14:44
51. 2 Cor. 11:30
52. Phil. 2:12

Chapter Six – In the Midst of Revival
1. Acts 8:21
2. 1 Pet. 2:2

3. 2 Tim. 4:2
4. 2 Cor. 3:3
5. Amos 8:11
6. Eph. 4:1-12
7. Ps. 133
8. Mark 4:1-8, Acts 18:25
9. Luke 3:1-14
10. Acts 2:37
11. Matt. 25:26-30
12. Luke 11:25
13. 1 Pet. 4:1
14. 1 Cor. 4:2
15. Col. 1:28-29 "We proclaim him, admonishing and teaching everyone with all wisdom, so that we may present everyone perfect in Christ. To this end I labor, struggling with all his energy, which so powerfully works in me." How few have "powerful" wisdom to deal with others that comes from God. Indeed, they barely have enough wisdom to get them through their problems – and this after having been in the Lord for years.
16. Ps. 18:33

Chapter Seven – The Revival Cry

1. Titus 2:7
2. Heb. 5:7-8 "During the days of Jesus' life on earth, he offered up prayers and petitions with loud cries and tears to the one who could save him from death, and he was heard because of his reverent submission. *Although he was a son, he learned obedience from what he suffered* . . . " (emphasis added)
3. 2 Cor. 13:11 (NIV)
4. Jer. 6:13-14
5. Mark 14:38
6. Isa. 40:30
7. Ps. 23
8. 2 Cor. 7:10-11
9. Gal. 5:25

10. Jude 1:20

CHAPTER EIGHT – WANTING TO HELP – THE OPPOSITION

1. Phil. 3:18
2. Luke 23:39, 1 Cor. 1:18
3. Acts 8:21, Eph. 5:1-7, 2 Tim. 3:1-5, 1 Cor. 5:11
4. Deut. 13:1-3

CHAPTER NINE – REVIVAL RESUMED

1. Ps. 22:6
2. 2 Tim. 1:8
3. Studying the Bible carries with it a deception. We are deceived when we study scripture unless we obey it. Beware that you are not deceived by your Bible study. See James 1:22.
4. James 1:4
5. Hab. 3:17-19
6. Rom. 8:28
7. Ps. 69:26
8. 1 Cor. 4:2
9. 1 John 5:13-15
10. John 15:7-8
11. 1 Cor. 1:18
12. Luke 20:18
13. 1 Cor. 11:28-31
14. Luke 10:21
15. James 1:27
16. Ex. 32:4-5 "He took what they handed him and made it into an idol cast in the shape of a calf, fashioning it with a tool. Then they said, 'These are your gods, O Israel, who brought you up out of Egypt.' When Aaron saw this, he built an altar in front of the calf and announced, 'Tomorrow there will be a festival to the Lord.'" (emphasis added)
17. 1 Cor. 5:9
18. James 1:27
19. Ps. 2:12
20. Rev. 12:4
21. Jer. 29:13

ENDNOTES

22. Heb. 12:11-14
23. Jer. 5:31, 6:14
24. Matt. 15:13
25. Rom. 7:18
26. Isa. 64:4

Chapter Ten – The Acid Test

1. 2 John 1:8
2. 1 Tim. 4:16
3. For example, men complain that we don't know what constitutes long and short hair. Therefore the command is not obeyed. However, to those with pure hearts God will give wisdom as to what He considers to be the correct hair length. Indeed, there would be unity among those who can hear from the Holy Spirit. See 1 Cor. 11:14-15.
4. Titus 1:16
5. Jer. 6:15

Chapter Eleven – The Whole Camp

1. Prov. 27:19
2. Luke 22:46
3. Luke 16:10
4. Col. 1:24 "Now I rejoice in what was suffered for you, and I fill up in my flesh what is still lacking in regard to Christ's afflictions, for the sake of his body, which is the church."
5. Luke 14:28
6. Luke 3:7
7. Luke 14:26
8. 1 John 2:15
9. 1 Cor. 7:29, James 1:27
10. 1 Cor. 7:27
11. Mark 7:27-28
12. Rom. 16:17
13. 1 Cor. 16:13
14. Matt. 5:23-24
15. 1 John 1:7

157

16. Isa. 58:13
17. 1 Tim. 2:12
18. 1 Pet. 3:21
19. Matt. 25:10-12
20. Ezek. 16:52

CHAPTER TWELVE – WORDS OF COMFORT

1. Luke 17:10
2. Amos 5:24
3. Prov. 18:2
4. Mark 5:26-34
5. 1 Cor. 1:10
6. Heb. 13:17
7. Col. 2:19
8. Luke 5:8
9. 1 Cor. 2:16 & 3:1-2

ORDER PAGE

Books

❑   A Whisper Revival $10.95

❑   Hating For Jesus $12.95

Sermon Tapes – Free – Choose one

❑   Luke 14 in 60 Minutes

❑   A Whisper Revival – The Sermon

❑   The Foundation of Love

ORDER FORM

Send the items checked above to:

Name_____

Address_____

City, State, Zip_____

Phone_____

Mail Order Form to:
WinePress Publishing
PO Box 428
Enumclaw, WA 98022

To order additional copies of

A WHISPER REVIVAL

have your credit card ready and call

(800) 917-BOOK

or send $10.95 plus $3.95 shipping and handling to

Books, Etc.
PO Box 4888
Seattle, WA 98104